Library of
Davidson College

The History of English Soliloquy
Aeschylus to Shakespeare

Lloyd A. Skiffington

UNIVERSITY
PRESS OF
AMERICA

LANHAM • NEW YORK • LONDON

Copyright © 1985 by

University Press of America,® Inc.

4720 Boston Way
Lanham, MD 20706

3 Henrietta Street
London WC2E 8LU England

All rights reserved

Printed in the United States of America

Library of Congress Cataloging in Publication Data

Skiffington, Lloyd A., 1925-
  The history of English soliloquy.

  Bibliography: p.
  1. Soliloquy—History. 2. English drama—History and criticism. 3. Shakespeare, William, 1564-1616—Technique. I. Title.
  PR635.S64S55   1985   809.2′45   85-5351
  ISBN 0-8191-4617-X (alk. paper)
  ISBN 0-8191-4618-8 (pbk. : alk. paper)

All University Press of America books are produced on acid-free paper which exceeds the minimum standards set by the National Historical Publications and Records Commission.

Untold thanks to Aida and Gail, who so painstakingly prepared the manuscript for printing.

Contents

Introduction		i
Chapter I: Classical		1
	Attican	1
	Roman	11
II:	The Mysteries	25
III:	Morality Drama	45
IV:	Shakespearean: Its Content	71
	Plot Exposition	73
	Homily	76
	Character-revelation (Psychological)	87
V:	Shakespearean: Structures and Language	99
	Two Lesser Known Structures	99
	Language	104
VI:	Shakespearean: Evolution Within	117
	Early Primitiveness	120
	Later Sophistication	125
	Selected Bibliography	133

Introduction

English soliloquy, born of Greek and Roman drama, nurtured on England's medieval stages, and ever so briefly leafed with gold by Shakespeare, is as a usable device for contemporary playwriting virtually dead. Reasons for its decline are summed up concisely in John Gassner's *Form and Idea in Modern Theatre*, where he treats of the nineteenth-century demand for near-photographic naturalism in stage settings, the insistence on the imaginary front wall on the stage: "It soon became apparent . . . that soliloquies and asides were not only generally unrealistic but actually breached the fourth wall."[1]

Because of the unquenchable popularity of Shakespeare and the Greek classics, however, soliloquy continues eminent on our twentieth-century stages and will not for one moment retreat to the wings. My purpose is to ferret out its classical sources, which are primarily Greek and Roman, and explore its six-hundred-years' reign in the theatre of England. The one exemption which may rightly be claimed in such exploration is the patent impossibility of an exhaustive treatment, and I claim that exemption. Shakespearean soliloquy alone is voluminous; the mass of medieval English soliloquy is far greater.

Despite such plethoric quantities, it is possible to demonstrate that Euripides' dependence on opening soliloquies reflects two centuries later in Plautus' formal prologues and two millenia later in Shakespeare's "starcrossed lovers" or "winter of our discontent" unfurlings. Such demonstrations of ancestral influence and neo-classical emulation provide prime reinforcement in my tracings of the evolution of English soliloquy.

"Soliloquy" is very often used interchangeably with "monologue."[2] The constant interchanging of the two terms frequently results in overlapped meanings. When is monologue not soliloquy? Is soliloquy always monologue? Clearly, one must set his own technical requirements for these two words. I use "soliloquy" to mean a locution dominating the stage and the attention of the theatre audience, delivered by a speaker who is alone on the stage.* Soliloquy is a type of monologue; the latter term is the generic

---

* To dispose of the one most prominent exception to my rule, Claudius is praying upstage and does not hear Hamlet's "Now might I do it pat" behind him; we may also assume Hamlet cannot hear the remorseful words of Claudius. (III.iii.73-96)

one. Distinctions between monologue and soliloquy are confined to a physical difference, the fact that the speaker of soliloquy is alone on stage.

The basic content of soliloquy is information. Plautus, for example, labeled many soliloquies and asides: "To the audience." Throughout my text, the assumption of Address to the Audience is primary, and its validity asserted. The informative content of soliloquy is various, and arbitrary labels — Plot Exposition, Homiletic, and Character-Revelation, for instance — conveniently, if not exhaustively, categorize the variety. Character-Revelation (i.e., Psychological) Soliloquy is a particularly useful designation for some of Shakespeare's more naturalistic soliloquies, such as Faulconbridge's acerbic musings on his new knighthood (I.i.182-216) or Macbeth's conclusion that ". . . function/ Is smothered in surmise" (I.iii.127-42).[3]

Notes

Introduction

[1] (New York: 1956), p. 30.

[2] *Webster's Eighth New International Dictionary* defines soliloquy as
> 1: the act of talking to oneself: a discourse made by one in solitude to oneself — monologue. 2: a poem, a discourse, or an utterance of a dramatic character that has the form of a monologue or gives the illusion of being a series of unspoken reflections.

Monologue is said to be
> 1a: a dramatic scene in which one person soliloquizes b: a dramatic sketch performed by one actor 2: a literary composition written in the form of a soliloquy 3: a long speech uttered by one person while in company with others.

A reason for the frequent interchanging of these two words can be seen in the two definitions: There is some overlapping of the definitions. The words "soliloquy" and "soliloquizes" are used in the definition of "monologue," and soliloquy is equated to monologue in the first meaning given for "soliloquy."

[3] All quotations from Shakespeare's plays are from G. B. Harrison, ed., *Shakespeare: The Complete Works* (New York: 1968), hereafter referred to as "Harrison."

Chapter I

Classical

Attican

Most devotees of drama find the apogee of English soliloquy fixed in Shakespeare. But an irreversible if ever so imperceptible evolution led up to those eloquent heights. This growth was seeded in Attican drama and sprouted in the Roman, and after lying fallow for many centuries shot up with new vigor in medieval England's mysteries and moralities. Finally, sloughing off the mediocrity of the Transitional Drama, soliloquy burst into unprecedented brilliance with Shakespeare. Thus Shakespeare's stirring soliloquies, certainly the best known of all, some of them doubtless the best of all, did not bloom starkly out of uncultivated literary sands; they are the brightest flowering of a garden nurtured in eras long before the Elizabethan. The process is still evident now and then in the modern theatre, but near demise. This chapter deals with the classical forerunners, establishing or asserting connections between their soliloquies and eventual English forms, medieval, Tudor, and Elizabethan.

For introductory purposes, a convincing example of such connections can be noted in Gilbert Murray's parallelism entitled "Hamlet and Orestes: a study in traditional types," where Murray stated and demonstrated with several references to his own translations:

> ... he [Orestes] indulges freely in soliloquies; (*I.T.* 77-94, *El.* 367-90; cf. *I.T.* 940-78; *Cho.* 268-305 and last scene): especially, like Hamlet, he is subject to paralysing doubts and hesitations, alternating with hot fits.[1]

Further, Professor Murray quoted a segment of an Orestes soliloquy and noted a striking similarity to one from *Hamlet*:

> How if some fiend of Hell
> Hid in God's likeness spake that oracle? *El.* 979[2]

Compare this fragment, as did Murray, to Hamlet's

> The spirit that I have seen
> May be the devil. (II.ii.627-28)

Focusing full attention on fifth-century Attican drama discovers the first firm, concerted seeding of soliloquy. With the choragos fully and irrevocably separated from the chorus, a natural and inevitable outgrowth of that separation occurred; the custom of formal set speeches by the choragos (which had usually, not always, taken the form of prologue) evolved into speaking responsibilities for individualized personae and, almost at once, soliloquies here and there, as first Aeschylus, then his renowned contemporaries, supplemented choral song and movement with portrayal of action and emotion through "actors."

It is somewhat commonly agreed that in the prior century Thespis had introduced prologues and the first "actor" into choral performances. However, prologues are scattered through near-Eastern literatures of much greater antiquity than the Greek, though not of course as actors' speeches, the main object of this study. Spoken by a presiding official or precentor, often in combination with a summons to sacrificial food and libation, these introductory invocations were a standard component of both ancient and Classical worship, and according to many authorities the basic form of prayer therein. As Theodor Gaster says in *Thespis* (New York: 1950), p. 71 (a work, despite title, not directly concerning itself with that sixth-century figure at all), such prologues developed "out of a more primitive ritual formula (prorrhēsis) which served originally, like the Sanskrit *nandi*, not to introduce the characters but to inaugurate the religious ceremonies at which the play was performed." While this survey of the evolution of English soliloquy does not, and would only be swollen if it did, pretend to uncover exhaustively the most ancient sources of solo speaking in drama, a brief excursus into a sampling of the ritualistic poetry of the Canaanites, properly viewed as typical of countless pre-Classical prologues, will serve to re-emphasize momentarily the utterly recondite origins of prologues per se.

The following prologue, from a Canaanite text known as the Poem of Dawn and Sunset, was inscribed on a clay tablet unearthed at Ras Shamra in 1930. (Gaster makes clear, by the way, on p. 228 of *Thespis*, the unremarkable nature of this ascribed poem title, pointing out that *dawn* and *sunset* — Šhr and Šlm — are common words in the Semitic pantheon.) This invocation provides the beginning of Part I of the poem, now entitled The Ritual. A similar prologue opens Part II, The Sacred Drama, its first words virtually identical to the ones cited here from Part I. Gaster avers that the ritual and dramatic portions are to be taken together as "the libretto of a religious performance," (*Thespis*, p. 225) i.e., the order of service for the Canaanite spring festival of firstfruits, predecessor of the Israelite Pentecost. The excerpt is from the words of a single speaker, and is introduced by the locution "*I* will invoke" *[iqra, iqran]*. Gaster continues: "Moreover, the single speaker into whose mouth the prologue is placed in the Canaanite text answers exactly to the Sanskrit *sūtradhāra* and the Greek *chorēgos*, i.e. the priestly 'presenter' of the sacred pantomime" (*Thespis*, p. 71). The passage follows:

2

> I would call on the two gods, comely and fair, even the
>   Prin[ces]:
> let honor be rendered to those celes[tial beings],
> . . . .
> let a [crown be set] upon their heads
> and plac[ed upon th]eir brows!
> Ho! eat of the viands,
> and ho! drink of the foaming wine!
> May peace reign, oh, may peace reign,
> ye sacristans and votaries! (*Thespis*, pp. 239-40, citing the transliteration of C. H. Gordon, *Ugaritic Handbook*, Rome, 1947)

As for the particulars of Gaster's theory that the *Poem of Dawn and Sunset*, the other dramas of its approximate epoch, and several of the Greek classical tragedies represent "drama derived from a religious ritual designed to ensure the rebirth of the dead world" (Foreward, p. vii), i.e., a "seasonal pattern of drama and ritual" (passim), such concerns must regrettably be left to studies other than the present one. However, further structural similarities exist between the Canaanite poem and fifth-century Greek drama. There is the presumption of a chorus of young men playing lyres, singing and performing a round dance in the earlier work, while its prologue features the honoring and describing of the goddesses (this serving also to introduce part of the action), and the greeting to the assembled worshipers (i.e., audience). Evolving radically from prayer to satire, this last element endured to be reproduced in livelier prologues of later millennia. Witness, for instance, many a declamation of puckish Plautus, or the fourman Presenter in Jonson's *Every Man Out* Induction. (The last includes an oaf named Prologue!)

To return to fifth-century poets, the principal consideration of this section, hardly had they initiated the division of dramas into individualizing roles than they began to make use of solo declamations. But in the hands of Aeschylus and his peers, soliloquy was far removed from the ritualistic prayer-prologues of earlier centuries. In the fifth century, soliloquies — whether situated as prologues or elsewhere in the plays — were put into the mouths of individualized personae, not mere Presenters. It remained for medieval and (rarely) Renaissance English drama to refurbish the role of Presenter as speaker of the prologue. For the Greeks, a character important to the action introduces the plot, explains the action, or, occasionally, describes characters, the last usually in third-person narratives but, in rare instance, as secular Greek drama continued to flourish, through soliloquies delineating the speaker himself to some degree.

Several examples of the two fundamental fifth-century types of soliloquy, plot-exposition, and character-description, and of variations from within them, are offered later in this chapter. And as will be further demonstrated in subsequent chapters, they have remained to this day two of the three basic types, the third — homily — having been born essentially of Roman drama in the second century B.C. Plautus may be termed father of the homiletic declamation. He employed it in virtually all of his comedies, though not always in the serious mode of English successors, having often burlesqued it to further his comic ends. An overall examination of Plautus' uses of soliloquy will be forthcoming in the next section; homiletic soliloquy will be examined, as applicable, throughout this study.

Among the dramatists of Athens, even the conservative Sophocles made use of soliloquy, although structuring his works more austerely than Aeschylus and far more so than the notoriously innovative Euripides. Sophocles employed only two soliloquies in the seven dramas surviving him, one each in *Electra* and *Ajax*. His reticence in applying this innovation to replace choral passages may well have served as contributing factor to the praise given him by Aristotle on one occasion, who in Chapter 18 of the *Poetics* appears to laud such conservatism in technique: "The chorus too must be regarded as one of the actors. It must be part of the whole, and share in the action, not as in Euripides but as in Sophocles."[3] Continually in Sophocles' works, as similarly in those of Aeschylus, where soliloquies are found in three of the seven extant plays (one in each), the chorus is the main vehicle for conveying information to the audience. Euripides, in contrast to both contemporaries, relied heavily on soliloquy to keep the audience informed, specifically through prologues in each of thirteen tragedies and the single satyr drama *(Cyclops)* of his nineteen surviving plays. (Some count only eighteen, and exclude the *Cyclops*.) Questions arising here as to whether this is unrealistic emphasis on percentages, given the relatively small proportion of plays now left to us from Sophocles and Aeschylus, are effectively obviated by another statistic, the practice of Euripides in positioning every one of his soliloquies as a prologue. Aeschylus opened two of his known plays, *Agamemnon* and *Eumenides*, with prologues, Sophocles none; as is apparent from the figures here, no surviving drama of the three contains more than one soliloquy. Incidentally, Aeschylus did not escape the barbs of Aristophanes, who in *The Frogs* took issue with such an effusion of prologues as he saw in the combined output of Euripides and Aeschylus (rather unfairly putting down Aeschylus, it would seem), and depicted the two playwrights making light of one another's prologues during their literary combat in Pluto's underworld.

Aeschylus' *Prometheus Bound* may well contain the earliest known soliloquy in author-attributed Western drama; it is surely one of the first. The date is uncertain: the Loeb Classical Library edition sponsors the opinion that the play was to be placed "either between the *Persians* [472 B.C.] and the *Seven* [467 B.C.] or between the *Seven* and the *Orestea* [458 B.C.]," while George Thomson, in *Aeschylus and Athens* (New York: 1967), p. 176, calls the *Prometheus* "probably the last of all." Fairly near the beginning of the play, Prometheus is lamenting his torture and agony. He is alone, and says so. Entering directly afterwards, the Chorus of Oceanides tells the audience it is entering — "We come" — as immediately prior to Prometheus' declamation Hephaestus and Strength have declared that they themselves were departing, effectively isolating the soliloquy.

> O thou bright sky of heaven, ye swift-winged breezes, ye river-waters, and multitudinous laughter of the waves of ocean, O universal mother Earth, and thou, all-seeing orb of the sun, to you I call! Behold, what I, a god, endure of evil from the gods.
> Behold, with what shameful woes I am racked and must wrestle throughout the countless years of time apportioned me. . . . All that is to be I know full well and in advance, nor shall any affliction come upon me unforeseen. My allotted doom I needs must bear as lightly as I may, knowing that the might of Necessity brooketh no resistance. . . . I hunted out and stored in fennel stalk the stolen source of fire that hath proved to mortals a teacher in every art and a means to mighty ends. Such is the offence for which I pay the penalty, riveted in fetters beneath the open sky.
> Ha! Hold! What murmur, what scent wingeth to me, its source invisible, heavenly or human, or blent of both? Hath there come to this crag at the confines of the world someone to stare upon my sufferings — or with what intent? Behold me, an ill-fated god, immanacled, the foe of Zeus, me who have incurred the enmity of all who resort unto the court of Zeus, by reason of my too great love for mankind. Ha! What's this? What may be this rustling stir I hear again hard by, of birds? The air whirs with the light rush of pinions. Whatever approaches is fraught with alarm for me. (11. 88-125)[4]

As with soliloquies of all eras, this one is a compound of purposes, effects and categories. Its opening ("Behold, what I, a god, endure of evil . . . .") may be included under Wolfgang Clemen's classification of lament soliloquy.[5] The main body of the declamation describes the persona who is speaking, revealing his life history and prognosticating his future. The central portion rudimentarily approaches delineation of character, in Prometheus' determination to "bear as lightly as I may." It is replete with ironies of situation ("fire . . . a means to mighty ends . . . the offence for which I pay the penalty . . . .") — reminiscent of the laments of Shakespearean kings on the burdens of those who would serve humankind (e.g., *III Henry VI,* II.v.2-54, and *Henry V,* IV.i.247-301). The speech closes with what may be labeled plot-exposition soliloquy, its moment of suspense ("this rustling stir") on the arrival of the chariot-borne Oceanides. Here, then, in one of the very first soliloquies of attributable Occidental drama, appear many of the uses and classifications found for all subsequent soliloquy. Homily, a very important part of Roman, medieval and Elizabethan soliloquy, is absent, reflecting of course many a philosophical divagation between Hellenism and the later cultures, not to mention the moralistic nature of Christian drama. However, in all the centuries since Aeschylus, only a few other distinctive elements of soliloquy have appeared, most of them stemming from the unparalleled originality of Shakespeare. None of those noted in Prometheus' utterance has suffered discard or disrepute over the long run.

In Aeschylus' *Agamemnon*, the watchman fills the entire opening scene with a soliloquy providing the background story for the drama. Not sufficiently memorable for quotation here, his words foreshadow action, imply intrigue, create suspense, revealing Troy fallen and Agamemnon returned. Near the close of the speech, the watchman also performs a brief dance before disappearing into the palace, not to appear again in the action.

The *Choëphoroe* contains no soliloquies, but the *Eumenides* opens with the Pythian prophetess delivering a soliloquy at the temple of Apollo. She recites first the sacred history of the shrine she is facing, then the terrible picture of bloody-handed Orestes now praying within while all but smothered by the sleeping Furies, a horror from which she has just now recoiled on entering the holy edifice. Here is soliloquy again performing an abundance of functions: prologue, suggestions of terror and of intrigue, stimulation of audience anticipation. Two millennia later, Shakespeare on occasion opened plays with choruses, prologues, or presenters, in one instance using the major character in opening soliloquy (Gloucester's "winter of our discontent"). On their departing the boards, stage business may not have been expected of these Elizabethan prologuers, but the purposes of their utterances directly parallel those of the Athenian's watchman and prophetess.

Providing fillip to the study of Aeschylus' works in this context, *The Seven*, winning or sharing first prize in 467,[6] contains a lovely prayer by Eteocles to Zeus for the safety of Thebes. It is not soliloquy — the citizens of Thebes are present — but it is a remarkable example of formal yet to-the-point diction and ably illuminates the character of Eteocles, further motivating agreement with Murray, who says, "He is, if I am not mistaken, the first clearly studied individual character in dramatic literature."[7]

Sophocles wrote soliloquies into only two plays now extant, *Ajax* and *Electra*, the former probably the earliest of the seven [c. 442/441 B.C.] and excerpted here. Following his humiliation in the contest for Achilles' armor, and alone on the seashore of Troy, Ajax positions and describes the sword (gift from Hector) for his suicide, praying now for a quiet death, and for first tidings of it to reach his brother Teucer. He petitions the Furies to

6

seek out his enemies, and Apollo to disclose his demise to his parents. And, finally, having said farewell to the earth and addressed himself to the nether world, Ajax falls on the sword and collapses behind shoreline sedges. After Ajax' declamation, the first of the two divisions of the chorus enters the scene and resumes the continuity of the drama.

[AJAX alone on the sea-shore, planting his sword in the ground.]

The slayer standeth where his stroke is sure;
If I have time to muse thus curiously.
The gift of Hector erst my foeman-friend,
The man most hateful to my soul and sight;
Now fixed in foemen's land, the land of Troy;
Fresh edged upon the iron-fretting stone,
Here have I planted it and set it fast,
A friend to help me to a speedy death.
My part is done; for what remains, O Zeus,
First I invoke thine aid; and claim my due;
'Tis no excessive boon I shall demand.
I pray thee send some messenger to bear
To Teucer the sad tale, that he may come
To lift me where I lie a bleeding corpse,
Fallen on this gory sword, lest I be first
Discovered by some enemy and cast forth,
A prey to dogs and birds. Thus much, O Zeus,
I crave of thee; and Hermes I invoke,
Born guide of spirits to the nether world,
To lay me soft to rest at one swift gasp,
Without a struggle, when into my side
I plunge this sword. Ye too I call to aid,
Maidens immortal, with immortal eyes
Beholding all the many woes of man,
Swift-footed hounds of vengeance, mark ye well
How by the Atridae I am all undone.
Swoop on them, Furies, blight and blast them both
In utter ruin, as they see me now!
On, ye Avengers, glut your maw, spare not,
Let ruin seize the whole Achaean host!
And thou whose chariot climbs the steep of heaven,
When in thy course thou see'st my father-land,
Draw in thy gold-bedizened rein and tell
My aged sire and mother of their son,
His sorrows and his end. Poor mother! when
She hears the tale, her piercing wail will ring
Through all the city. But how profitless

> These idle lamentations and delay!
> With such despatch as may be let's to work.
> O Death, Death, Death, draw nigh and look on me—
> Yet there below I shall have time enow
> To converse face to face with Death. But thee,
> O bright effulgence of this radiant day,
> On thee, the Sun-god charioteer, I call
> For the last time and never more again.
> O light! O sacred soil of mine own land,
> My Salamis! my home, my ancestral hearth!
> O far-famed Athens, race akin to mine,
> Ye Trojan springs and streams, ye plains of Troy,
> Farewell, ye nurses of my fame, farewell!
> This is the last word Ajax speaks to you.
> Henceforth he talks in Hades with the dead.
>
> *He falls upon his sword.*
> Re-enter CHORUS. (Sophocles, II, pp. 69-73)

Perhaps of all the soliloquies composed by the Greek triumvirate, this one in its effect most resembles Shakespeare's finest soliloquies of character-revelation. It reveals Ajax' character ennobled by the manner of his suicide, the ignominy of defeat thus obliterated. It shows him calm in the face of death ("My part is done . . . ."), careful only for his family (". . . tell/My aged sire and mother of their son . . . ."), and reverent toward his gods ("O bright effulgence of this radiant day . . . ."). Given his reputation as mere strutting cock, it may well be observed that "nothing in his life became him like the leaving it." Of course, this reassessment of Ajax, this attempt to restore him in the world's eyes, is Sophocles' main point in the play.

Near the beginning of Sophocles' *Electra*, the title-character utters a soliloquy comprising lament and prayer. It does not stand comparison with the declamation of Ajax cited above, since it is predictable, if not wholly formulaic, in its tone of mourning and its plea to the Erinyes and other forces to avenge her father's death. Only through its subject-matter would this outcry ever be likely to call to mind such agonizing avowals of vengeance as those of Hamlet, for example.

Euripides, as mentioned earlier in contrast to his principal peers, left to the world by far the greatest number of soliloquies. And little wonder he was taunted by Aristophanes for a superfluity of prologues; each of his fourteen extant soliloquies is the opening speech for a play. His *Hippolytus* is introduced by Aphrodite, who summarizes the background of the plot and forecasts much of what is to come. In *Medea*, the nurse's opening soliloquy performs the same functions; she recapitulates the story to date and foreshadows the terrible wrath of Medea. *Electra* offers a prologue by the peasant husband of Electra, who therein fully informs the viewers as to events ensuing. This speech also limns the peasant as gentle and altruistic, poor but high-born, nobly refraining from possessing the woebegone wife vengefully wedded to him by Aegisthus. *Iphigenia in Tauris* is unfolded by the aggrieved daughter's recounting her own story up to the point of the play's first action. Dionysos gives prologue to *The Bacchae* with the history of his life and of the legend forming the basis of the drama, and he brings on the chorus of Theban women, whom he has latterly been distracting, by hailing them just before exiting. Jocasta fills an almost exactly identical purpose at the outset of *The Phoenician Maidens* by delivering to the audience in soliloquy the legend of Oedipus before she departs from view. And so on, in eight other plays of the dramatist, even the *Cyclops*, which commences with a comic soliloquy by Silenus, reviewing a bit of the legend-plot and establishing his place within it.

It is doubtless self-evident, as emphasized by Lane Cooper on p. xiv of his introduction to *Fifteen Greek Plays* (transl. G. Murray *et al.*, New York: 1943), that "the diction of Euripides is closer [than that of Aeschylus and Sophocles] to the language of conversation." There can be little doubt that felicity in colloquial idiom furnished one important reason for Euripides' constant reliance on prologue-soliloquy, since, ancient or modern, prologues are commonly among the most colloquialized portions of drama, and those of Euripides are not exceptions to this practice. Quotation from the peasant's prologue to *Electra*, at least that part which delineates him through his own modest words as poor in gold but noble in manhood, is in order here, to illustrate the conversational qualities of language showing forth from Euripides' writing in spite of the fact of translation, or whatever the identity of the translator, qualities proclaiming themselves in virtually any available version:

> Noble my blood is, but in this world's goods
> I am poor, whereby men's high descent is marred, —
> . . . .
> But never I — Cypris my witness is —
> Have shamed her couch: a virgin is she yet.
> Myself think shame to take a prince's child
> And outrage — I, in birth unmeet for her[.]
> Yea, and for him I sigh, in name my kin,
> Hapless Orestes, if to Argos e'er
> He come, and see his sister's wretched marriage.
> If any name me fool, that I should take
> A young maid to mine home, and touch her not,
> Let him know that he meteth chastity
> By his own soul's base measure — base as he.
>
> (*Euripides*, II, p. 9) (11. 37-38, 43-53)

Affording a side note, Euripides' *Cyclops* is apparently the only extant satyr-drama attributed to any single author. However, Gilbert Murray asserted, on p. 8 of his introduction to *Aeschylus, The Suppliant Women* (New York: 1935): *"The Supplices,* produced some time between 499 and 472 B.C., is still in the main a simple religious celebration, with no individual characters, and almost no plot." And on p. 9 of the same: "Thus the *Supplices* is extremely close — much closer than critics have suspected — to the original choric or communal dance out of which tragedy arose. It consists in the manoeuvring or interaction of three Choruses and their leaders ...."

Finally, Euripides, generally considered the least conservative of the three Athenians, may have been indeed the one most bound by tradition in two or three specific ways. As shown earlier, the prologue is a most ancient device, descended from ritual and drama centuries older than those of the fifth century. But it was Euripides, not the more lyrical Aeschylus or the august Sophocles, who positioned every one of his fourteen soliloquies as prologue to its piece. By itself, that fact might be neither here nor there. However, other more arresting parallels to his primitive forebears appear in the plays of Euripides. As Gaster says in *Thespis*, p. 70, "Indeed, if the long and beautiful chorus, *Bacchae* 64-169 be compared carefully with the ritual Paean to Dionysus discovered at Delphi, it will be found that it reproduces not only the general tenor and sentiment of the latter, but also almost all of its standard clichés and technical terms. Similarly, a choral ode quoted by Porphyry from the lost *Cretans* of Euripides turns out, once again, to be but a poetic elaboration of the canonical Dionysiac chant."[8] Gaster is pressing the point that both Euripides and the Canaanite writers worked into their literary dramas the standard hymns of the much older seasonal festivals from which they evolved. In Euripides' continual use of prologue appear both a tidbit of relationship between classical Greek soliloquy and its ancestry and stunning evidence of tradition binding two plays of the most radical dramatist of the age.

Further grist for Aristophanes, the other five dramas of Euripides also contain prologues, though not precisely in soliloquy form: the *Heracleides* opens with Iolaus delivering what in every respect amounts to a soliloquy except for the fact he is sheltering Hercules' sons in his arms at that moment. In *The Madness of Hercules*, Amphitryon and Megara share an information-prologue, as do Hector and the chorus in *Rhesus*. For the *Suppliants*, Aethra declaims the prologue to the chorus; in *Aulis* Agamemnon recounts his legend-story in reply to leading questions by the Old Man.

Finally, even Aristophanes himself, his complaints about contemporaries notwithstanding, was not totally exempt from the burgeoning custom — *The Clouds* (prod. 423 B.C., much earlier than *The Frogs*, 405, which, like *The Birds*, 414, offers no soliloquies) contains a soliloquy, comic of course, but a prologue no less. The father Strepsiades is reciting the profligate horse-racing habits of Pheidippides, while that son is heard snoring beside him.

Soliloquy, then, came of age in the fifth century B.C., an early offspring of the speaking-role at first accorded only to the choragos. Appearing in Aeschylus and Sophocles only five times in total against fourteen for Euripides, none having placed more than one in a single drama, the device had achieved respectability and prominence well within its first half century of use. It had also evolved into two of its three permanent principal types, introduction to or foretelling of plot and/or action, and description of personae. The third, homily, did not rise to any definable importance until second-century (A.D.) Roman drama, there brought to bear on comedy by Plautus, next reviewed in this study.

Roman

Roman drama having achieved (and deserved) much less acclaim than the Attican, comparable regard is offered here. Brief concentration on only two of the best known Romans, Plautus and Seneca, will serve to review Roman soliloquy; few other Roman writers are important specifically to this section. Titus Maccius Plautus (254 B.C. - 184 B.C.), translating and adapting now often unidentified plays from New Comedy, engaged his characters constantly, voluminously, insistently in soliloquy, often puckishly — as when directing applause at the close — and sometimes even in song. Along with numberless soliloquies, Plautus continually featured asides, these too at times directing audience response. Prologues are abundant, formal epilogues less frequent, although, as noted, the comedy is closed on occasion by a line or two playfully urging approval. Like those of Euripides, Plautus' prologues often summarize the history behind action and character and enunciate the plot to come. However, as never with Euripides, they are usually comical, too, mainly no doubt to capture the inconstant attention of unlettered Roman viewers. In the twenty works extant (for some scholars twenty-one, including the hundred lines remaining of the *Vidularia*), lament is doubtless his most numerous single variety of solo speech, although he is far and away best remembered for merriment in soliloquy. In range of tone and topic he seems limitless, although this very versatility gives rise to occasional assessments like that of Gilbert Norwood on p. 4 of *Plautus and Terence* (New York: 1932): ". . . the offence that puts Plautus outside the pale of art . . . is his practice of tying together — not only in the same play, sometimes in the same scene — modes of feeling and treatment utterly incongruous."

Excerpt here from a soliloquy by Sceparnio, choleric old servant in *Rudens*, may suffice to show the ironic tone so often entertaining in Plautus' declamatory speeches, laments excepted.* This play was thought by F.A.

---

* Act/scene divisions, included for convenience of the reader, are those of later editors: it has not been firmly established that Plautus intended five acts in his plays.

Wright in *Three Roman Poets* (New York: 1938), p. 79, to have been adapted from *The Wallet* of Diphilus and first performed in 192 B.C. Foolish, surly, decrepit Sceparnio holds romantic hopes far beyond his social potential; the ironies implicit in the speech are more than faintly reminiscent of aspiring Malvolio:

> Ye gods above, I never dreamed
> I should be pleased an urn to fill! [for Ampelisca, the girl]
> . . . .
> Just fancy, at my time of life!
> Here I am thinking of a wife!
> . . . .
> Ah, she's in love with me as well:
> The rogue is hiding, I can tell. (II.v.entire)[9]

Ampelisca may indeed be hiding, but not, to be sure, for the reasons Sceparnio proffers. In the same comedy, acclaimed as the star of the piece by punning Plautus, Arcturus has already delivered a prologue written in the simple style of Euripides, consisting of a brief homily, (not much seen in Greek drama), followed by a bit of plot-summary. Then, in a six-line soliloquy at the onset of Act I, Sceparnio is heard grumbling about the storm-damage to his thatched roof. Soon, in I.iii, Palaestra cries out in a song of lament at having endured both shipwreck and loss of her friend, Ampelisca. The latter appears, and in turn as it were, opens the succeeding scene with her own plaintive song, further exemplifying how as in several other plays Plautus adroitly wedded drama and melody in *Rudens*. A valet, Trachalio, begins and closes II.ii with brief soliloquies summarizing plot-action; Ampelisca ends II.iii with a like declamation, and finishes the next scene with yet another. Quick on the heels of the soliloquy by Sceparnio excerpted above from II.v, Charmides concludes the act with one recapitulating his part in the plot; then Daemones introduces Act III with another describing a lately enjoyed dream. One after another to the end of the play, innumerable soliloquies ensue, even in epilogue.

Plautus' reliance on soliloquy is unrelenting throughout his plays. For instance, *Aulularia* contains a prologue by the household god, several other soliloquies, and many asides, while *Pseudolus* is introduced by a comic two-line prologue which cautions:

> You had better stand and stretch your loins: a play by Plautus,
> a long one, is now to be enacted.[10]

This latter play also features asides and additional soliloquies, as in the ending lines of Act I which heartily commend attention to the second act (p. 207) and a four-line epilogue by Pseudolus, who off-handedly calls for applause while inviting the audience to the next performance (p. 285). Interestingly, the only known flute solo in Latin drama appears in this play (1. 573a) where Pseudolus tells the spectators that the flutist will play for them while he, Pseudolus, is in the house forming a plan. On his reappearance, the meter has changed from the rhythm of matter-of-fact speech to that of rippling, multi-paused "song," suggesting that the musician has played a tune.

In the famed *Miles Gloriosus*, whose title suggests a role-type often inaccurately ascribed to Plautus' invention but unquestionably strengthened and rendered memorable by him, Palaestrio speaks what certainly amounts to a deferred prologue for the play, at the beginning of the second act. He turns to the audience, and, in true Plautine fashion, proceeds to parody all plot-summarizing prologues:

> I intend to do you the courtesy of outlining the plot of this play, if you will do me the kindness of listening. However, he who does not care to listen may arise and leave, so that there may be a seat for him who does. *(pauses, with a glare ready for fugitives)* Now as to the reason for your assembling in this place of mirth, I shall acquaint you with the plot and name of the comedy we are about to act. (*Plautus*, III, pp. 131 & 133)

The speech continues on for over two pages more, continuing also to make light of prologues which tell the story but itself admirably serving that very function. Interspersed throughout this comedy are soliloquies by various speakers, and several asides, among them a near full-page mockery, midway in II.ii, uttered by the old gentleman of Ephesus, Periplectomenus (inadvertently not named at this point in Nixon's English translation, but properly identified in his Latin text). This is an aside to outdo all others, explaining its own identity as an aside and then its intended service, as the old man describes in lightly mocking detail the sight-gag gesturings of the puzzled Palaestrio. A few lines:

> Think it out. I'll step over here in the meanwhile. [moving away and watching Palaestrio amusedly] Just look at him, how he stands there with bent brow, considering and cogitating. He's tapping his chest with his fingers. Intends to summon forth his intelligence, I suppose. Aha! Turns away! Rests his left hand on his left thigh, and reckons on the fingers of his right hand. Gives his right thigh a smack! A lusty whack — his plan of action is having a hard birth.
>
> (*Plautus*, III, p. 143)

Plautus' manipulation of the dramatic conventions of soliloquy needs mention here. The soliloquies previously cited hew to the definition of soliloquy delineated in the initial pages of this study; but Plautus was not always so fastidious. In *Aulularia*, for only one example, Euclio has just removed his treasure from his house to the safer temple of Faith. He comes forth from the shrine, and shouts before the audience:

> Only be sure you don't let anyone know my gold is there, Faith: . . . Oh my God, what a beautiful haul he would get, if anyone should find it — a pot just crammed with gold!
> (*Plautus*, I, p. 297)

Having led the spectators to believe this a soliloquy, Plautus then causes Strobilus, Lyconides' slave, to jump up and exclaim:

> Ye immortal gods! What's all this I heard the fellow tell of! A pot just crammed with gold hidden in the shrine of Faith here! . . . I'm going in there . . . . *(Ibid.)*

Even though it is assumed that interiors were never shown on Roman stages, that all the action took place in front of the houses, nevertheless, Plautus was taking raucous liberty here with audience expectations concerning overhearing, as he often did in other plays.

A word about satire. The term now occupies a much broader spectrum than it did for the Romans. It is freely applied nowadays to all incidental satire, such as the condescension shown by Periplectomenus to Palaestrio in the mocking speech cited above from *Miles Gloriosus*. Latin literature contains a great amount of such light scoffing, but the Romans would not have used the word *satura* as a generic term for most of today's applications. As J. Wight Duff indicates on p. 13 of *Roman Satire* (Berkeley: 1936), ". . . special words like *irrisio, illusio, vituperatio, insectatio, acerbitas, dissimulatio* . . . would be required to suit different passages." In addition, as Duff so aptly puts it on p. 14, "The ancients themselves were puzzled by the word *satura*: the moderns have not reached complete agreement on the problems involved." It is not practicable to enter into a prolonged discussion here on the origins of the word *satire*. The question is one of caution against too readily employing the word without regard for historical perspective on its usages.

Itinerant workman from the Apennine hills, "Titus of Sarsina" (later to be nicknamed "Plautus" — "flatfoot," or "splayfoot" — and still later "Maccus," i.e., Joey the clown) in Rome became successively actor, merchant, soldier, then, in middle age, playwright, perhaps even owner of rights in his plays. These uproarious plays burst forth uniquely comical on the brand new stages of Rome, especially constructed for each play, then taken down.[11] None such had appeared before him on that fallow literary scene, a handful of predecessors are now hardly remembered. Few save Terence and Seneca were to follow, and Terence, quiet, elegant stylist of the next generation, Caesar's *dimidiatus Menander*, was no successor to Plautus' comic genius. No Roman plays before or since displayed the good-natured fun, the cynical jibes or the poetical deftness of Plautus. In his own era he stands out even more than Shakespeare in his, given the paucity of skilled Roman playwrights and the plethora of accomplished Elizabethans.

During Plautus' youth, one Livius Andronicus had pioneered in introducing Greek drama to the Romans, presenting at the Ludi Romani in 240 B.C. a Greek play in Latin translation. As far as is known, no literary work had been composed in Latin before. In *The Roman Stage*, (London: 1950) W. Beare categorically states on p. 22: "He found Rome without literature or written drama." Cicero's several references to Andronicus' offering of 240 B.C. generally take precedence over Jerome's date of 187 B.C., but, either way, Plautus obviously inherited nothing like a full-fledged tradition of Roman drama. Indeed, save for Andronicus, Greek Epicharmus writing in Sicily, and Cnaeus Naevius, there is essentially only Plautus to consider in the Republic, let alone to draw from for complete plays. F.A. Wright asserts in *Three Roman Poets* (New York: 1938), p. 8, that "within a few years after 240 B.C. Latin literature and Roman comedy begins with Cnaeus Naevius." He adds that the fragmentation of Naevius' many play manuscripts, and the loss of his probable invention, the *fabulae praetexta* (plays about heroes of Roman history or legend), is "a grievous misfortune, for if we may judge from those scanty remains he seems to stand in the same relation to Plautus as Marlowe stands to Shakespeare." Plautus is virtually all that remains, with the minor though fascinating exception of comic traditions and types from the *Fabulae Atellanae*, viz. Maccus, stock clown figure, source of one of Plautus' names and of the Italian *Commedia dell' arte*, Punch and Judy, and the Marx Brothers as well. Excepting the comedies of Plautus, the Atellan plays were the only really popular form of drama that the Romans ever knew, continuing to be staged for centuries, until the pantomime-shows of the Empire obliterated all forms of spoken play. It is assumed, by the way, that the Plautine plays themselves received only a few successive performances originally, then came to be "archived" in some manner which helped insure their survival, and their revival in popularity after the death of Terence.[12]

That all of Plautus' extant plays are *palliatae*, adaptations of Greek originals, need not lessen one whit the estimation of his playwriting skills, especially his command of poetry and of the language of jest, and his intuition of the public taste. As Wright says on p. 26, ". . . by the constant use of assonance and alliteration as an integral element of poetry — a device than which nothing can be more Latin or less Greek — he completely transformed [the Greek meters]. His whole method of writing, indeed, is completely his own and owes nothing to any predecessor." And later (p. 29): "These songs [in Plautus' plays, sung to specially composed music for the double flute] mean nothing less than the invention of rhyme, something which even the Greeks did not know." W.Y. Sellar stated: "Plautus maintained the thoroughly popular character of Roman comedy, and poured a strongly national spirit into the forms which he adopted from Greece."[13] And Beare emphasizes, on p. 3 of the introduction to *The Roman Stage* (London: 1950): "The most obvious feature of Roman drama is its derivative character. All our Latin comedies are based on Greek originals, themselves now lost. It is plain, moreover, that the Latin plays are not exact translations; the translators omitted what they thought dull, added what they thought would interest their public and introduced other alterations of various kinds." Or, as succinctly put by H. E. Butler, on p. 23 of *Post-Augustan Poetry* (Oxford: 1909), "He [Plautus] had grafted the festive spirit of Roman farce on to the more artistic comedy of Athens."

A few possibly authentic fragments of Philemon's ninety-seven comedies are commonly suggested as indicating some of Plautus' sources, e.g., *Phasma* for the *Mostellaria* and *Emporos* for the *Mercator*; unfortunately, only the fragments (and approximately sixty titles) survive from Philemon. The *Stichus* is known to have been translated by Plautus from Menander; a few others, possibly only two, may have been. Other Greeks, among them Diphilus, have also been named. Regrettably, not one complete example of Greek New Comedy of the third century B.C. exists. Some fragments of Menander's plays, including one sober explanatory prologue (in *Perikeiromene*) quite unlike the boisterous rantings of many by Plautus, and a considerable collection of single lines or passages quoting Menander and contemporary dramatists, were discovered early in the present century. Otherwise, all that survives of New Comedy is in the rarely direct translations and dimly evident bases of reworked plots by Plautus and Terence. It is also by odd coincidence true that the first works of Latin literature to have reached us in finished form are the plays of Plautus, says Beare on p. 2 of his introduction. For certain, Plautus was one of a kind, in both chronological and artistic perspectives of soliloquy. Continuing the custom of prologues, but otherwise generally observing no models of declamation, no prior examples (despite the adaptive origins of the plays themselves), Plautus brought forth a singular brand of comical soliloquy, and steeped his comedies in one after another of them.

Founded in severe, dark chasms of Greek tragic poetry, soliloquy had thus evolved by the second century B.C. into a mainstay of raucous Roman comedy, declaimed by lively lord and strutting servant alike. Satire, not seriousness, had carried the day in the drama come down to us as most memorable of the Republic. Usually serious in content and tone, laments abound in Plautus, but burlesquing and cynicism preempt a far greater number of his soliloquies in line after line as in turn the plays confront us with soliloquy on soliloquy. Adding no novelty of species★ and little innovation in tone, Plautus nevertheless gave license to later legions of playwrights, especially in medieval England, who would cautiously emulate such

---

★ Asides, which Plautus included by the dozen, are for the purposes of this study considered as only an offshoot of soliloquy and not as a wholly distinctive entity.

floods of soliloquy in drenching their own works therewith, sometimes in unsuccessful emulations of his spirited ironies, often of course not knowing Plautus' plays at all. Some of these later effluxes will be examined in a later chapter.

Son of the famed rhetorician of the same name, narrowly escaping death for his own brilliant oratory in Caligula's senate, banished a near-decade on accusation of adultery with the Princess Livilla (not the first author so accused), and subsequently tutor to the young Nero, Lucius Annaeus Seneca ($c.$ 4 B.C. - 65 A.D.) — or the unknown author whose plays are attributed to him — is generally credited with having written the only Latin tragedies safely come down to the present. The Senecan plays have many a soliloquy, although by no means the number seen in Plautus, than whom probably no dramatist ever depended more thoroughly on the device. All but one of the ten tragedies of Seneca contain soliloquy. That one, *Thebais*, is patently unfinished; as Thomas Newton noted in his edition of 1581, "it neyther hath in it, Chorus, ne yet the fifth Acte."[14] All but three, *Thebais, Thyestes,* and *Oedipus,* open with a prologue by a leading persona, in the fashion of Euripides; in *Hercules Furens, Medea* and *Agamemnon,* the first act consists only of the prologue plus choral song. (In these brief acts, neither actor nor chorus addresses or is assumed to be aware of the other, somewhat parallel to Claudius' prayer of remorse before the unhearing Hamlet.) Of the seven with prologues, all save one, *Hippolytus,* exhibit other soliloquies as well, although the soliloquy by the Spirit of Achilles beginning the second act of *Troas* was added, likewise the Spirit, by the 1581 translator Jasper Heywood to that work he thought "unperfite, whether left so of the Author, or parte of it loste."[15] Incidental to this study is the long prominent opinion that Seneca's dramas were written not for stage performance but for private audiences. He may have shared the opinion of Ovid, expressed long after publication of the latter's *Medea,* that he too was not so depraved as to write for the public stage. As one of Rome's richest men, disclaiming all contact with plebeians or their diversions, he certainly is not likely to have lowered himself to composing performances for a theatre scorned by literary Romans. Although no coherent description of Roman theatre and drama has come down from those times, tragedy had in fact given way on the stage to pantomime, called by the Greeks the "Italian dance," introduced to Rome in 22 B.C. by Pylades and Bathyllus. Privately presented or not, the tragedies attributed to Seneca are the only complete Latin tragedies available for perusal. And whatever the arena of presentation, the effect of Seneca's soliloquies on the audience would surely have been the same.

Too lengthy to permit full quotation here, and too typical to require it, Thyestes' oration at the outset of the *Agamemnon* dominates the opening and displays several of the rhetorical mannerisms of Seneca adjudged excessive by the present age. The speech occupies over half of the first act, which is filled out with a song of the chorus. The act is very brief, however, as are many in Seneca; such divisions into acts represent the work of editors, not of the author, who in his exhibited preference for four choral odes in a play may or may not have been adhering to the Horatian dictum that a play could not be successful unless it contained five acts. The word "act" is, by the way, a misnomer in these tragedies; action is most often only recounted, not depicted. The plays, moreover, artificial imitations of Greek tragedy, were undoubtedly meant to be declaimed or read, not acted. Cloaked in the antique charm of 1581, the first eight lines of Thyestes' soliloquy follow:

> Departinge from the darkned dens which Ditis
> low doth keepe,
> Loe heere I am sent out agayne from Tartar
> Dungeon deepe,
> Thyestes I, that wheather coast to shun doe
> stande in doubt,
> Th' infernall fiendes I fly, the foalke of
> earth I chase about.
> My conscience lo abhors, that I should
> heather passage make,
> Appauled sore with feare and dread my
> trembling sinewes shake:
> My fathers [sic] house, or rather yet my
> brothers I espy,
> This is the olde and antique porche of
> Pelops progeny. (p. 101)

No doubt most notable of all the characteristics typical of Seneca within this excerpt is the amount of emphasis on darkness, deep dungeons, and dread. Depiction of the speaker as secretly watching his ancestral home, beset by grievous doubt and pursued by foul fiends, is particularly and thoroughly Senecan, sponsoring an aura of abhorrence and intrigue historically so influential as to be thought in eras much subsequent peculiarly "medieval," still later "Elizabethan." In its issuance from the son-soiled maw of Thyestes, and in its tone of "trembling sinewes" and of other horrible insinuations, the speech more than a little echoes elements in *Titus Andronicus*.

Thyestes' lament of anguish, his in-flight account of the journey, and his review of the legend behind the action furnish description of character and introduction of plot, the two principal types of audience information come down to the Empire from Greek drama. Homily, a third and then more recent major category, primarily Republican in origin, emerges in at least one soliloquy by Seneca, that of Hippolytus opening the tragedy of that name. Essentially like all moral exposition, it is a hymn to the prowess and largesse of the god, accessible to mortals on proper behavior. The deity in this case, Diana, controls all hunted wild creatures and, her precepts observed, assures sylvan success even to lowly boar-hunting husbandmen. Excerpts follow from near the end of the lengthy soliloquy of Hippolytus:

> Graunt good successe unto thy mate, Virago,
>   thou Divyne,
> That secret desartes chosen hast for noble
>   Empire thyne:
> . . . .
> To thee the Tygar fierce his divers spotted
>   breast doth yeeld,
> The rough shaghatry Bugle turnes on thee his
>   backe in field,
> Eke salvage Buffes with braunched hornes:
>   all thinges thy quarelles feare,
> . . . .
> If that the Ploughman come to field, that
>   standeth in thy grace,
> Into his nettes the roused beast full sure he
>   is to chase.
> No feete in sunder breake the coardes and home
>   he bringes the Bore
> In jolting wayne, when as the houndes with gubs
>   of clottered gore,
> Besmeared have their grymed snoutes: and
>   then the Countrey rout
> To Cottages repayre in rankes, with triumph
>   all about.
> Lo, Goddesse graunt us grace: the hounds
>   already opened have,
> I follow must the Chase: this gainer way
>   my paynes to save,
>   I take into the woods. (pp. 138-39)

"Virago" bears the older meaning of strong, large, manlike woman — here, goddess of men's sport, the chase. "Mate" refers to Hippolytus' vow to serve the chaste Diana, forbearing mortal woman's love to follow the gentlemanly life of hunting, a career cut off of course in its prime by the wrathful wish of Phaedra.

A homily much more direct in dichotomizing virtue and vice forms the choral epilogue to *Hercules Oetaeus*. Exempt from examination as soliloquy, it is mentioned only to show that the homiletic lines in *Hippolytus* are not in themselves unique in Seneca's plays, although he rarely moralized in soliloquy itself. It is important to note here that the *Oetaeus* presents many problems bearing on authorship, not the least of which is a double chorus. The question of authenticity cannot be fully covered here; some assurance, if not resolution, may be taken from such statements as Butler's on

p. 42 of *Post-Augustan Poetry* (Oxford: 1909) that "its general resemblance to Seneca in style and diction is too strongly marked to permit us to reject it [a considerable amount of the play] *en bloc*."

An interesting incident from the life of Seneca dispels belief that he was capable of writing only sober-sided works. On p. 91 of *Roman Satire*, J. Wight Duff remarks that "to find the staid philosopher L. Annaeus Seneca (*ca*. 4 B.C. - 65 A.D.) also among the satirists has so startled some scholars that they have solved their difficulty by denying . . . his authorship of the *Apocolocyntosis* or "Pumpkinification" of the Emperor Claudius, in which Claudius is ejected from heaven and sent back by way of earth to Hades. This is, however, to ignore manuscript testimony and, as far as style goes, to overlook the capacity for humor . . . besides his skill in verse writing as seen in his tragedies . . . ." Butler labels the *Apocolocyntosis* "an example of the *Menippean Satire*, that strange medley of prose and verse" (p. 33n).

Like Euripides and Plautus before him, Seneca made much use of prologue-soliloquy; like the latter he interspersed soliloquies widely within his plays. Unlike Plautus, whose "acts" run considerably longer and often display several soliloquies, Seneca often filled most of a brief act with a single declamation. He contributed little, if any, originality of form to the continuing evolution of soliloquy, but content was a different story: Seneca's soliloquizers emphasize tribulations and horrors, and recount them while in their very grip. Much more than predecessors, Greek or Roman, Seneca constantly played on the impact of darkness and dread, doubt and despair, intent on theatrical effect and phrasing a grandiloquence now dismissed as melodramatic, quaintly archaic. As for homily, it was rare with him; displays of distress and pleas of lament were Seneca's forte. Caligula himself, as reported by Butler (p. 4), may have had the last word on the weaknesses of the style, describing Seneca's rhetoric as "commissioned," and "'sand without lime.'"

The name of Seneca has furnished the epithet applied alike by Elizabethans and moderns to a type of rhetoric consisting of what Milton Kennedy, on p. 10 of *The Oration in Shakespeare* (Chapel Hill: 1942), calls "primarily declamation and display." Butler (p. 179) also speaks of "the rhetoric of display that culminated in Seneca and Lucan [Seneca's nephew]," and later (p. 187) of "the brilliant rant of Lucan and Seneca." "Bombast" is undoubtedly the most popular name for Seneca's set speeches, often lyrical nonetheless, but Kennedy's "display" may be more accurate, though by far less convenient for those who would make Seneca a scapegoat for medieval and Elizabethan excess. Furthering the less accusatory perspective, Charles T. Prouty writes in his introduction to the Crofts Classics edition of *The Spanish Tragedy* (New York: 1951), p. vi: "Perhaps the chief charm of Seneca lay in his infinitely polished rhetoric . . . . Such a style was well-suited to the taste of a decadent Rome and it also suited the taste of Englishmen who were just becoming aware of the glories of language."

Numberless volumes of literary criticism in recent centuries have rendered it unnecessary and unrewarding to explore more fully at this juncture the distinctive qualities of Seneca's rhetoric. Sufficient for the moment are two opinions from the late-sixteenth-century edition out of which the Thyestes soliloquy is drawn, which exhibit vividly the reverence for Senecan discourse prevailing throughout the decades prior to 1600. Jasper Heywood, "Fellow of Alsolne Colledge in Oxenforde" and translator of *Thyestes* and *Troas* in Thomas Newton's 1581 edition of Seneca's ten plays, praised in his introduction to *Troas* "the flowre of all writers, Seneca" (p. 3). Beare informs (p. 228) that earlier, in 1551-52, the *Troas* had been performed to approving audiences at Trinity, Cambridge. Editor Newton himself, in his dedication of the book of tragedies to Sir Thomas Henneage, wrote glowingly of Seneca's "peereless sublimity and loftinesse of Style" (p. 5). It remains for ensuing chapters here (III and VI especially) to bear out the importance to English soliloquy of Seneca's theatricality and sense of intrigue, and of more general aspects from his rhetoric and style.

Notes

Chapter I

[1] *Proceedings of the British Academy, 1913-14,* 4th Annual Shakespeare Lecture (London: 1914), p. 393.

[2] *Proceedings of Brit. Acad.,* p. 393.

[3] *Aristotle The Poetics, "Longinus" On the Sublime, Demetrius, On Style,* Loeb Classical Library, ed. E. Capps, T. E. Page, and W. H. D. Rouse (London: 1927), p. 71.

[4] *Aeschylus,* I, Loeb Classical Library, ed. E. Capps, T. E. Page, and W. H. D. Rouse (London: 1930), pp. 225 & 227. All subsequent Greek soliloquies are taken from this Loeb series.

[5] *English Tragedy Before Shakespeare,* trans. T. S. Dorsch (London: 1961), Ch. xiv and passim.

[6] *The Seven Against Thebes,* Oxford Univ. Press series, trans. Gilbert Murray (New York: 1935), Introd., p. 9.

[7] *The Seven Against Thebes,* trans. Gilbert Murray, Introd., p. 19.

[8] The Porphyry reference is sourced by Gaster from *De abstin.* iv, 19, p. 172: transl. by G. Murray in Jane Harrison, *Prolegomena to the Study of Greek Religion* (Cambridge: 1921), p. 479.

[9] *Plautus: Rudens and Other Plays,* Broadway Translations Series, trans. F. A. Wright and H. L. Rogers (London: n.d.), p. 86. The references to *Rudens* in this paragraph are also from this source.

[10] *Plautus, Vol. IV,* Loeb Classical Library, trans. Paul Nixon (London: 1950-52), p. 151. Subsequent citations from Plautus are from this Loeb series. W. Beare, *The Roman Stage* (London: 1950), p. 151, says that this prologue seems to be post-Plautine.

[11] Margarete Bieber, *The History of the Greek and Roman Theater,* 2nd ed. rev. (Princeton: 1961), p. 168.

[12] W. Y. Sellar, *The Roman Poets of the Republic,* New ed., rev. and enl. (Oxford: 1881), p. 156.

[13] Sellar, p. 156.

[14] *Seneca, His Tenne Tragedies Translated into English,* ed. Thos. Newton (1581; rpt. Bloomington, Ind.: n. d.), p. 99. Quotations from Seneca are from this source.

[15] *Seneca, His Tenne Tragedies,* p. 4.

Chapter II

The Mysteries

To speak of English soliloquy evolving as an unbroken stream of traditions, emulations, and occasional remarkable changes would of course be grossly inaccurate. Medieval drama, liturgical or secular, English or Continental, saw new beginnings in soliloquy, with little or no indebtedness to the wondrous classical past. As writings worthy of the name *play* (as distinguished from the diminutive tropes of the preceding three centuries) began to appear, though infrequently, in the thirteenth century, the early writers soon enough discovered the need for solo speeches in their works. But it was a discovery original with them, independent of the Greek and Roman forebears whose dramas remained virtually unknown to them. By notable coincidence, soliloquy was born again, engendered by the same stage necessities which had prompted Euripides and Plautus. Most of the types known earlier in classical drama were reborn. A few varieties not evident on the Greek and Roman stages appeared, such as sermons and command-to-quiet prologues, to name only two.

Between Seneca's Rome and medieval England twelve centuries of drama lie hardly explored, barely explorable. During all that time, sweepingly labeled as the Dark or Early Middle Ages, dramatic forms seem to have undergone little or no evolution, and, common estimate has it, shockingly little practice. Nevertheless, theatre there was; vestiges have been unearthed.

Probably chief among the centers of spectacle early within the Christian epoch was Byzantium, its liturgic drama intimately connected with the *acta* of the people, the folk-drama of the Hippodrome. In the latter, fragments of the traditions of the earlier Greek theatre were maintained and continued, though not its literature. Attired in theatrical garb and divided into choruses, the participants in the Hippodrome sang, under orchestral lead, the praises of the emperor. And around 900 A.D., Patriarch Theophylactus, brother-in-law to Emperor Constantine VIII, introduced the professional actors and dancers of the Hippodrome into St. Sophia.[1] This mixing of secular show and religious trope continued unaltered for centuries, assuredly observed by crusaders in the armies of occupation.

The first mysteries in Western Europe were written subsequent to the first crusade. This fact suggests that soldiers of the crusades (plus of course pilgrims and a few itinerant merchants), exposed to the spectacles and dramatized rituals of Byzantium, became the conduit for liturgical drama to their homelands, given the ostensible religious motivation for their presence in the Near East in the first place. Voltaire, and innumerable others, have found in Constantinople the origins of the ritual play and the mystery, findings certainly difficult to refute.

In any case, very little is known, or seemingly knowable now, of soliloquy in those long past ages. Yet dramatic dialogue did then exist. The earliest ecclesiastical drama of Byzantium is quite possibly that of the hymnist Romanus. A few generations after Chrysostom and Basil, Romanus wrote a Nativity poem containing not only the story of the Birth but also a dialogue among the Wise Men, Mary and Joseph, in what may be described as a mystery five centuries older than any known from the West. In the history of the world compiled for the emperor Constantius, certain Syrian cities were compared, with Tyre and Beirut said to supply the best actors, Gaza the finest declaimers.[2] Historically, where dialogue in drama has arisen, soliloquy has inevitably appeared soon after. Further suggestion of soliloquy in Byzantium exists, recondite yet strongly indicative. Fanatical early Christians having proclaimed that the devout should not read works of ancient pagan authors, the angered emperor Julian retorted by proscribing such readings, and school attendance as well, for Christians. The trained sophists and grammarians Apollinarius (father and son of the same name) then began what may have been the first conscious attempt to write Christian drama. Hoping to negate Julian's prescription of illiteracy, the two writers remolded stories from Scripture into tragedies as near like those of Euripides as possible and comedies like Menander's. The pair were subsequently condemned for heresy for their efforts, and called by one contemporary "Arians" merely because they had introduced the theatre into the church.[3] Plays in the mode of Euripides or Menander could hardly have been free from soliloquy, those two Greek masters having served as chief models of soliloquy for so many authors in so many later eras.

This sad episode of the Apollinarii is but another demonstration of the continuing cycles of association and divorcement of drama and religion. Despite its birth in religious rite in early Greece, and its having undergone earlier, separate generation in ritual of Near Eastern cultures, how many times drama has brought its authors nothing better than death for heresy, and has figured in struggles to cleave it from its theological parentage. Witness the Inquisition, the attempt of the Council of Trent (1543-63) to abolish liturgical drama from the service-books, the ban in 1548 by the French Parliament on the production of sacred drama by the lay *confrérie*, and the closing of the English theatres by the Puritans. Both sides in such clashes have undoubtedly sought justification in the words of Paul (I Cor. iv.9), from which "spectacle" is often translated as "theatre": "For I think that God hath set forth us the apostles last, as it were appointed to death: for we are made a spectacle unto the world, and to angels, and to men."

As iterated above, when drama appeared in Europe after the hiatus of dark centuries, it was engendered anew. Classical tragedy had last been acted in Byzantium in the first century; comedy had utterly degenerated into buffoonery, from thence having died in Rome under clerical proscription. Entertainers continued to move about on the Continent, chanting the French *chansons de geste* or declaiming the Arthurian *contes*, acting out the characters from their tales. But they had inherited virtually nothing from classical theatre, and brought forth nothing worthy of the appellation *play*. Even Dante named his great poem a *Commedia*, Chaucer his *Troilus* a tragedy, neither scholar seeming much concerned, if at all, that these terms had once been the province only of the drama.

Early medieval soliloquy, essentially that of the so-called mysteries, is completely and exclusively an offering of information to the audience, as were its classical equivalents. This information is of two basic sorts, exposition of plot, and homily, the latter inevitably offered only as appendage to the other. The expository falls naturally into two sub-categories, soliloquies of plot-action and of role-action. In plot-action soliloquies, a speaker reveals or recapitulates the plot of the piece, in part or in its entirety; in role-action soliloquies a player describes or predicts his own physical actions. Medieval soliloquy at times includes rudiments, nothing more, of a third basic type of information, i.e., character-revelation, "psychological" soliloquy intended either to reveal motivation or to display the workings of inner turmoil in a personality (as opposed to an abstraction-persona) at war with himself. Its ultimate basis lies in medieval soliloquies of speaker-identification and in the psychomachic *debat* of the morality. It remained for Shakespeare to design, almost single-handedly, that which is now generally called psychological soliloquy, or character-soliloquy. It will be noted in a subsequent chapter (VI), by the way, that Shakespeare's dependence on the structure and materials of medieval soliloquy is roughly equal, at least quantitatively, to his innovating in soliloquy. (The word "character," in the phrase "character-soliloquy," indicates character only in the psychological sense, not "character" meaning a role or part in the play.)

Most of medieval soliloquy has a charmingly ingenuous quality, which results from both the obviousness of its informative intent and its naiveté in language, and points up the absence of any connection with the stateliness and elegance of classical forebears. Often in the cycle plays dialogue, as well as soliloquy, is both descriptive and expository, performing its own audience-informing services. Such speeches insist with great seriousness that the audience note the persons of the play and their identities or qualities, and sometimes inadvertently — and, by present standards, quite naively — reveal such facts of performance as, for instance, that children are playing the Angel roles. "Naiveté" is not necessarily a pejorative here, however, as T. S. Eliot's observation concurs: "Certainly it is a relief to turn back [from the Senecan bombast of some of the early Elizabethan dramatic poetry] to the austere, close language of *Everyman*, the simplicity of the mysteries . . . ."[4]

The charm now seen in the ingenuousness of medieval soliloquy is largely the result of the movement toward naturalism in drama over the several centuries. Yesterday's modernity has become today's antiquity. The hoariness of venerable age now covers soliloquy written in the Middle Ages, and the perspective of centuries causes the present age to view most of the ancient efforts as quaint, primitive, and unsophisticated. It may well be that forgetfulness presently dominates in regard to the highly contrived nature of some of nineteenth- and twentieth-century soliloquy, which in some later era will also seem quaint and ingenuous.

Soliloquy of notable structural or theatrical importance to plays does not appear in England until the thirteenth century, and then in only a very few of the manuscripts now extant. The scarcity of manuscripts from the mid-thirteenth century to the mid-fourteenth, characterized by E. K. Chambers as a period transitional between liturgical and secular drama (*The Mediaeval Stage* [Oxford: 1903], II, 69), may date partly — if not largely — from the wholesale destroying of liturgical books at the Reformation. At any rate, despite the small number of soliloquies available now even from the fourteenth century (mainly from the Chester and York cycles), several new conventions in soliloquy arose in those two centuries, such as the prologue command-to-quiet from the monarch or his messenger, and soliloquies bearing plot-exposition and sermon together. Another important convention, the parading of the prophets, also made its appearance, continuing highly in evidence in the fourteenth century, although sometimes not through soliloquies but simply in a line of players filing on to speak their successive monologues.

Under the Angevin kings England shared much in the drama emerging in northern France at the beginning of the thirteenth century, especially plays from Arras, these latter signaling the new emancipation of French drama from clerical control. As the court moved back and forth across the Channel, likewise clergy and minstrels, there resulted a considerable importation of both liturgical and popular drama, both kinds produced and acted by lay drama guilds, the *puys*. Jehan Bidel's *Le Jeu de Saint-Nicolas* (Arras, c. 1200), wholly secular in its settings of Arras streets and taverns, furnishes instance of soliloquy so early in English dramatic history as to be disputably either English or French, written in French but brought to England when two vernacular languages existed side by side.

Le Jeu de Saint-Nicolas opens with the soliloquy in question, a prologue of approximately one hundred lines. Delivered by the "preacher," and referring to the night of performance as St. Nicolas' Eve (5 December), the prologue is both sermon and description of the play-plot to come. The following lines from its conclusion display its outstanding aspect, visible not in its content per se but rather in its intimacy of address to the audience, an intimacy much more characteristic of Plautus than of the Elizabethans to come, although allied to neither, and quite typical of medieval soliloquy, by the way:

> Pour che n'aiés pas grant merveille
> Se vous veés aucun affaire;
> Car canques vous nous verrés faire
> Serra essamples sans douter
> Del miracle representer
> Ensi con je devisé l'ai. (11. 106-11)
> (And so do not be too much amazed
> if you see some funny business here;
> for whatever you see us doing
> will be a faithful attempt, it's certain,
> at representation of the miracle
> just as I have recounted it.)[5]

The stage represents a boundless kingdom containing several disparate focuses of action; the Saracen's palace, the prison, and the tavern are a few. Roughhewn pleasures ("funny business") are depicted throughout the play — drinking, gambling, and more, a veritable ("faithful") history of Arras low life. Nonetheless, this particular very early prologue is sibling to, if not parent of, the line of sermon-prologues so prominent in fourteenth- and fifteenth-century English drama. It certainly projects the tone of familiarity of address so widespread in that later epoch, possibly serving as one progenitor of that tone.

An untitled play from Cambridge and the so-called Rickinghall fragment exhibit two other thirteenth-century verse prologues. Both have Anglo-Norman and English versions, for use in different parts of the country; speaking English or French was determined by locale as well as by occupation or wealth. The Cambridge prologue is spoken by the messenger of "the emperor," who commands silence in the name of the emperor and of Mahomet. The Rickinghall fragment is delivered by a *rey coronné* who voices his own command to quietude. Excerpt from the Cambridge verse-prologue follows:

> S'il i a nul que noyse face,
> V que entre en cet[e] place
> Pur nostre iu ren desturber,
> Prendre le frun saunz demorrer
> E jucer ley[n]s en la prisun. (11. 9-13)
>
> If ani his so hardi man
> þat stille ber him ne can,

> ф'amperur hat þat men awonge
> And so uyt him men anhonge,
> . . . .
> And hym bete and sore swenge. (11. 11-14, 18)

(If anyone here makes noise/or enters into the acting place/to disturb our play for any reason,/we shall have him taken without delay/and thrown into the prison. (11. 9-13, in the Anglo-Norman above)[6]

This imperative quite patently became a convention. *Pride of Life*, recently dated mid-fourteenth century, opens with a similar prologue, where the audience is exhorted to pray for the weather to shine on the outdoor performance and ordered that they "distourbith noȝt oure place" (1. 110).[7] In *Duk Moraud* (c. 1400), a story of incest, Duk Moraud vaunts at the beginning:

> No yangelyngys ȝe mak in þis folde To-day; (11. 8-9)[8]
> (yangelyngys = quarreling, chattering, lit., jangling)

possibly to keep out non-paying spectators. The command-to-quiet continued to be employed many times in the cycle plays (as by Herod or his Nuntius in Wakefield Plays XIV and XVI, by Pilate in XX, and by Octavian and his messenger in Chester Plays VI).

The twelfth-century play of *Adam (Ordo Repraesentationis Adae)*, written in Anglo-Norman French and quite possibly produced in England,[9] since Norman French was still the official court tongue, offers a very early example of parading the prophets. It deserves examination here as a possible ancestor of prophet-soliloquy in the cycle dramas, but on its own, too, for inventiveness in multi-level staging and felicity in relating exalted themes to audiences of ordinary people. The levels of the stage apparently extended from the church door, with the top of its steps representing both Heaven and Paradise, to a large acting space at the bottom, the *platea*, surrounded by the audience. This vernacular play is very long, and one after another Abraham, Moses, Aaron, David, Solomon, Balaam, Daniel, Habakkuk, Jeremiah, Isaiah, and Nebuchadnezzar, each in verisimilar costume and seated on a bench, speak their prophecies. Following each declamation, devils lead the prophet to hell, presumably off through the audience via a hell-mouth. The manuscript is incomplete, so we cannot know how many prophets might have come after Nebuchadnezzar, or whether the drama might have continued with the full story of the life and death of Christ, as did the cycle plays later.

The procession of prophets which follows the staged murder of Abel expound on the connection between the Old and New Testaments, uttering prophecies interpreted in the Middle Ages as foretelling the birth of Jesus. Source for this procession *(Ordo Prophetarum)* was a famed medieval Christmas sermon, the *Sermo contra Judeos, Paganos, et Arianos de Symbolo*, erroneously attributed to St. Augustine. In that sermon, prophets from the New Testament and from pagan antiquity join Old Testament patriarchs in testimony pointing out the stubborn failure of the Jews to note the evidence of the advent of Christ.[10] Abraham does not appear in the *Sermo*, but is the first prophet to speak in the play. He, like some of the succeeding prophets, is introduced to the audience by a Figure representing God, who reads aloud the opening of the *Sermo*:

> You, I say, I do summon before a tribunal, O Jews.

Then Abraham speaks his soliloquy, in language which in the French is possibly even more plain and down-to-earth than in the English translation given here:

> I am Abraham, such is my name.
> Now listen to my entire message:
> Let him who has good hope in God
> Hold to his faith and his trust.
> He who will have firm faith in God,
> God will be with him, this I know
>   through personal experience.
> He tested me, I did his pleasure;
> Well I accomplished his will.
> I would have killed my own son for him,
> But by Him I was told not to.
> I would have offered him for a sacrifice;
> God turned me from it, in his justice.
> God has promised me — and true indeed it will be —
> Another such heir will come of my lineage
> Who will conquer all his enemies;
> Thus strong and mighty will he be.
> He will hold their gates in his hands,
> And their castles; he will be no serf.
> Such a man will issue from my seed,
> Who will commute our sentence of damnation,
> And by whom the world will be ransomed.
> Adam will be delivered from his pain;
> The peoples of every nation
> Will receive benison through him.
>   (11. 745-768)[11]

Followinng the sermon-prophecy, the devils come and lead Abraham to hell, and Moses assumes the speaking-place and delivers his homily, much briefer than Abraham's; the several prophecies are of various lengths.

It is of course impossible to credit a single play as the main forerunner of such processions in the cycle plays, because the cycles vary so notably in presenting the transition from Old Testament to New. The York cycle, for instance, renders its *Prophetae* in narrative instead of dramatic form, the Wakefield has an incomplete one, and the N Town exhibits a mixing of Old Testament prophets with a long series of personages from the line of Jesse, including kings in the genealogy of Christ, in all, twenty-seven figures. In the Chester cycle the speeches are ordinarily monologues, not soliloquies, and the procession presents textual difficulties, being apparently a late emendation, and found in only one of the five manuscripts (Harl. 2124), where it is inserted into the Balaam-Balak episode before that episode is finished. The play of *Adam*, though centuries earlier than the cycles, arguably affords a dramatically superior and more refined example of the procession, especially for scholars of soliloquy.

The York cycle, dated by its medieval editor as mid-fourteenth century and recorded as first performed in 1378, includes a soliloquy type probably originating in that century, the Satan-soliloquy. In the opening lines of *The Fall of Man* (Cowpers), Satan is seen rationalizing his planned attempt to defeat God's purpose in Eden by tempting Eve, miffed that God has taken upon Himself the nature of man, not that of the angels, Satan's erstwhile affiliation. The "rationale" follows:

> For woo my witte es in a were!
> That moffes me mikill in my minde:
> The Godhede that I sawe so cleere,
> And parsaived that he shuld take kinde
> Of a degree
> That he had wrought, and I denied that
>   aungell kinde
> Shuld it nog[h]t be.
> And we wer[e] faire and bright;
> Therfore methoght that he
> The kinde of us tane might,
> And therat dedeyned me.
> The kinde of man he thoght to take,
> And theratt hadde I grete envye;
>
> (11. 1-13)[12]

In his final two lines (23-24), Satan, approaching Paradise, tells the audience he is about to put on serpent guise and try blatantly lying to Eve. The prologue is of interest among its kind chiefly because of the unusual argument advanced by Satan to defend his machinations. Satan-soliloquies are visible in numerous plays of the four cycles, as in the lament of Lucifer at the end of the incomplete manuscript of *The Creation and the Fall of the Angels* (Wakefield), or the long prologue to the N Town *Passion Play*, Part I, where, "gorgeously attired," Satan exemplifies Pride, through his boastful words and vain apparel. Interestingly, the Fall of Satan is not found in Genesis. Only a few passages of the Bible seem to allude to it, some of them vaguely, such as Isaiah 14:12 (an invocation to the morning star). Revelation 12:7-9 tells of a war in heaven in which Michael and his angels cast to earth the serpent Satan and his angels. In Luke 10:18, Christ says (only this once in the New Testament) that he saw Satan falling from the sky. These scant references form the basis for the medieval Church explanation of the origin of evil in the universe. Evil thus came after the creation of angels — via Lucifer's disobedience — and prior to the creation of man.

The York *Birth of Jesus* (Tille Thekers, i.e., Tile Thatchers) exhibits yet another convention, deserving mention but not quotation here, contemplations by Mary and Joseph at Jesus' birth. Early in the play Mary is shown in joyous soliloquy, worshiping her babe as "Lord God" in lines tender in diction and fairly closely derived from Scripture, a derivation typical in this convention. Outside the stable, gathering firewood, Joseph is heard, after a routine exposition segment, realistically expressing surprise at the Star's sudden shining.[13]

Conventional contemplations by Mary and Joseph are also heard in the York *Flight into Egypt* (The Marchallis, i.e., Marshals, horse tenders, shoesmiths). Joseph's prologue-soliloquy, again apparently staged outside the stable where Mary tends the child, reveals considerable feeling; he is dedicating himself to serve God in caring for the child. Mary's lines, however, are merely predictable. A little later on, Joseph has another soliloquy, not so original, praying for protection from Herod's death sentence on the male children.

In the Wakefield *Annunciation*, Joseph is given two soliloquies. The first finds Mary in a stage situation somewhat parallel to that of Hamlet overlooking Claudius' soliloquy of remorse; she is visible to the audience but obviously not hearing the words of Joseph as he pours out his thoughts. The story of the Annunciation in this drama, incidentally, is not based on an account from the New Testament, but on the Apocryphal Book of James (Protevangelium), xiii.

Jesus is of course featured as a speaker of soliloquies in many medieval plays, as in *The Woman Taken in Adultery* (N Town), for instance, where He is represented as giving the prologue-homily. This play, by the way, contains four asides, something of a rarity in medieval drama. *The Harrowing of Hell* (Wakefield) opens with Jesus in an expository soliloquy; *The Resurrection of the Lord* and *The Last Judgment* of this cycle also reveal Him in soliloquy, spoken in the latter from "Heaven," apparently a scaffold above the "stage."

The N Town *Passion Play* has two Christ soliloquies worthy of note, in their poignant maturity of expression. In Part I, Jesus cries out to His God for deliverance from the Cross, in language capable of moving the most agnostic soul. A portion follows:

> O Fadyr, Fadyr! for my sake
> This gret Passion thou take fro me,
> W[h]ech arn ordeyned that I shal take
> Yif mannys sowle savyd may be.
> And yif it behove, Fadyr, for me
> To save mannys sowle that shuld spille,
> I am redy in eche degre
> The wil of the[e] for to fulfille.
>
> (11. 917-24)[14]

The plaint is thrice interrupted by Christ's going to awaken Peter; a sweet tenderness lends the plea originality despite its close adherence to Scripture. In Part II, a similar originality shines through from the brief introspective soliloquy of Peter following his three-time denial of his Leader:

> A, weelaway, weelaway! Fals hert, why whilt thou not brest,
> Syn thy maistyr so cowardly thou hast forsake?
> Alas, qwher shal I now on erthe rest,
> Til he of his mercy to grace wole me take?
>
> I have forsake my maister and my Lord, Jhesu,
> Thre times, as he tolde me that I shuld do the same.
> Wherfore I may not have sorwe anow,
> I, sinful creature, am so mech to blame.
>
> Whan I herd the cok crowyn, he kest on me a loke,
> As who seyth, "Bethinke the[e] what I seyd before!"
> Alas the time that I evyr him forsoke!
> And so wil I thinkyn from hens evyrmore.
>
> (11. 193-204)[15]

In both tone and subject matter this lament of Peter is echoed in *Antony and Cleopatra*, within the soliloquy which so deftly helps delineate the noblesse of Enobarbus:

> I am alone the villain of the earth,
> And feel I am so most. O Antony,
> Thou mine of bounty, how wouldst thou have paid
> My better service when my turpitude
> Thou dost so crown with gold! This blows my heart.
> If swift thought break it not, a swifter mean
> Shall outstrike thought. But thought will do 't, I feel.
> I fight against thee! No, I will go seek
> Some ditch wherein to die, the foul'st best fits
> My latter part of life. (IV.vi.30-39)

Following his excellent detailed explanation of the above N Town passion sequence, David Bevington, on p. 478 of his *Medieval Drama* (Boston: 1975), acclaims as another noteworthy feature of its production "the use of meditative lament, or soliloquy, to offset scenes of tumultuous action." He cites Christ's sermon on the Eucharist at the Last Supper, and Mary's grief-stricken lament when Christ is being dragged around the arena toward the chief priests. Although these are indeed touching speeches, they are not, by the criteria of the present study, soliloquies, since the Disciples are present at the Supper, and Mary is sorrowing in company with Mary Magdalene.

A very distinctive sort of soliloquy, no doubt intended to be taken seriously when first presented on pageant stages, is the rantings of Herod, a convention widely exercised in thirteenth- to fifteenth-century drama. A prime example of the type is found in the Wakefield *Herod the Great*, in the sequence on the Slaughter of the Innocents. In the prologue, Herod's Nuntius, speaking in the nine-line stanza of the Wakefield "Master" which is seen throughout the play, has declared the great worthiness and puissance (and, indirectly, the tyranny) of his king. This herald, a non-Biblical character, has severely warned the audience about Herod, but, when the potentate arrives, fawns upon him. Herod's rant closes the play, revealing him to be as described everywhere in medieval drama: cowardly, bullying, murderous, mercenary, unspeakably tyrannical, and, in this particular utterance, threatening bodily harm for the slightest inattentiveness. He even promises the audience a reward "when I com again" (1. 467), although his soldiers, in a prior line (434), have indicated his hypocrisy in such offers: "So have ye lang saide — do somwhat thertill!"[16] In the soliloquy Herod boasts of the Slaughter of Innocents, claiming a uniquely memorable fatality list — 144,000, he says. There are numerous comic touches by the "Master," including Herod's closing admonition — from him, of all people — "Bese not to[o] cruell." (1.511) following directly on his warning of the breaking of brains! Some of the vituperations are cleverly original, too. The slaughter itself, preceding the soliloquy in the play, is one of the most gruesome, shocking episodes in all religious drama.

The Wakefield *Second Shepherds' Play* is classified by custom as a mystery play, but it is certainly a worldly one, and it offers relatively mature characterization of its personae in contrast to most mysteries. In its secular sophistication, this play is probably superior to the other mystery dramas cited in this chapter. Indeed, the secular dramatic elements dominate and nearly submerge its religious content. Dating from the second half of the fifteenth century, according to Chambers (*The Mediaeval Stage*, II, 412), the play bears a framework of comedy: the situation as a whole is farcical, and there is comedy of character in the interaction between Mak and the shepherds and in Mak's "southern accent." From out of the Roman mime tradition, coarse farce is a dramatic format even older than the medieval drama, and the *Second Shepherds' Play* exemplifies the description by Karl Young on pp. 8-9 of his Introduction to *The Drama of the Medieval Church* (2 vols., 1933; rpt. Oxford: 1951): "Indecency was mingled with morality. ..."

The play is full of soliloquies, most of them grumblings of the shepherds concerning working conditions, horrible weather, and the tribulations of the married state. But midway in the piece is one illustrating the two principal types of information in mystery soliloquy, exposition and homily. It is spoken by Mak, the sheep-stealer:

> Now were time for a man that lakkys what he wold
> To stalk prevely than unto a fold,
> And neemly to wirk than, and be not to[o] bold,
> For he might aby the bargan, if it were told
> At the ending.
> Now were time for to reyll;
> Bot he nedys good counsell
> That fain wold fare weyll,
> And has bot litill spending.
>
> Bot abowte you a serkill, as rownde as a moyn,
> To I have done that I will, till that it be noyn,
> That ye lig stone-still to that I have doyne;
> And I shall say thertill of good wordys a foyne:
> "On hight,
> Over youre heydys my hand I lift.
> Outt go youre een! Fordo youre sight!"
> Bot yit I must make better shift
> And it be right.
>
> Lord, what thay slepe hard! That may ye all here.
> Was I never a shepard, bot now will I lere.
> If the flok be skard, yit shall I nip nere.
> How! drawes hederward! Now mendys oure chere
> From sorow.
> A fatt shepe, I dar say;
> A good flese, dar I lay.
> Eft-whyte* when I may,   *Repay
> Bot this will I borow. (269-295)[17]

Mak addresses the audience softly ("prevely"), in what is primarily a soliloquy of role-action; at the moment that he is casting a spell on the shepherds ("abowte you a serkill") and stealing a sheep, he is telling the audience exactly what he is doing ("That may ye all here."). The obligatory homiletic factor in mystery soliloquy appears in Mak's words early on about the need for "good counsell," although the counsel he has in mind may not be divine.

This Wakefield play opens with a soliloquy by the First Shepherd,

Coll, who is exclaiming over the dreary lot of shepherds in general, abused and overtaxed by the gentry. Coll speaks:

> Bot we sely husbandys that walkys on the moore,
> In faith, we ar nerehandys outt of the doore.
> No wonder, as it standys, if we be poore,
> For the tilthe of oure landys lyis falow as the floore,
> As ye ken.
> We ar so hamyd,
> Fortaxed and ramyd,
> We ar mayde handtamyd
> With thise gentlery-men.
> Thus thay refe us oure rest, Oure Lady theym wary!
> These men that ar lord-fest, thay cause the ploghe tary.
> That, men say, is for the best; we finde it contrary.
> Thus ar husbandys opprest, in po[i]nte to miscary
> On life.
> Thus hold thay us hunder;
> Thus thay bring us in blonder.
> It were greatte wonder
> And ever shuld we thrife. (11. 10-27)

These few lines display the relative sophistication of the entire long speech. They reflect its social comment on the exploitation of the poor by the wealthy ("Thus ar husbandys opprest"), as well as a plaintive realism of diction ("outt of the doore," "handtamyd") worthy of epochs much later in English drama. In the solo grumblings of Coll can be seen embryonic beginnings, possibly the birth, of character-soliloquy, skillfully leavened by comedy. By no means does this feeble medieval foray represent a full-fledged achievement in character-soliloquy for its anonymous writer; nevertheless, the attempt resulted in a near-miss, a hint of things to come. To be sure, the three shepherd roles do offer somewhat more than the usual run of stereotypes in mystery drama, but they offer so much less of psychological dimension than most characters in Shakespearean drama that the grumblings about taxes, weather, and marriage remain only the plaints of shepherd-stereotypes, not of "persons" on the stage.

There is instance of soliloquy unmistakably homiletic in *Abraham and Isaac* (c. 1470-80 for this MS; the original may date back to the fourteenth century). Used here is the Brome version, so called because the MS was found in Brome Manor, Suffolk. (The Chester Cycle also contains a strikingly similar *Abraham and Isaac*.) On the final page of the play, a Doctor (scholar) enters to address the audience with what amounts to an epilogue for the piece. It is an epilogue with a moral, however, and may in fact be termed a sermon. Abraham and Isaac have entered their tent; the speech is addressed to the assembly, not to the father and son:

> Lo! sovereyns and sorys, now haue we schewyd,

> Thys solom story to gret and smale;
> It ys good lernyng to lernd and lewyd,
> And þe wysest of vs all,
> Wythowtyn ony berryng.
> For thys story schoyt ȝowe [her]
> How we schuld kepe to owr po[we]re
> Goddys commawmentys wythowt grochyng.
>
> Trowe ȝe, sorys, and God sent an angell
> And commawndyd ȝow ȝowre chyld to slayn,
> Be ȝowre trowthe ys ther ony of ȝow
> That eyther wold groche or stryve therageyn?
>
> How thyngke ȝe now, sorys, therby?
> I trow ther be thre ore a fowr or moo;
> And thys women that wepe so sorowfully
> Whan that hyr chyldryn dey them froo,
> As nater woll, and kynd;
> Yt ys but folly, I may wyll awooe,
> To groche aȝens God or to greve ȝow,
> For ȝe schall neuer se hym myschevyd, wyll I know,
> Be lond nor watyr, haue thys in mynd.
>
> And groche not aȝens owre Lord God,
> In welthe or woo, wether that he ȝow send,
> Thow ȝe be neuer so hard bestad,
> For whan he wyll, he may yt amend.
> Hys comawmentys [sic] trevly yf ȝe kepe wyth goo[d]hart,
> As thys story hath now schovyd ȝow befor[n]e,
> And feytheffully serve hym qwyll ȝe be qvart,
> That ȝe may plece God bothe euyn and morne.
> Now Jhesu, that weryt the crown of thorne,
> Bryng vs all to heuyn-blysse! (11. 435-65)[18]

The opening eight lines of the soliloquy fulfill both a dramatic function and a homiletic one. They praise the importance of the play, "good lernyng"; very briefly summarize the content of the play ("For thys story schoyt . . ."); and reveal the moral of the piece ("How we schuld kepe to our po[we]re/ Goddys commawmentys wythowt grochyng"). The second segment (the subsequent thirteen lines) poses a challenge to the faithful as to which ones would begrudge their own offspring to God, answered by the speaker in ironic phrasing ("I trow ther be thre ore a fowr or moo"). This middle segment closes with a detailing of the moral lesson of the first segment, that "Yt ys but folly" to begrudge entire obedience to God. The final ten lines of the soliloquy declare the possibility of reward for unbegrudging service of God's commandments ("For whan he wyll, he may yt amend."), exemplified in God's climactic reward to Abraham for his unexceptionable faithfulness. Finally, throughout the speech a demonstrative emphasis is apparent. The verb "show" appears three times, twice in the opening segment, and once near the end of the soliloquy. This is the ultimate basis of mystery soliloquy, to "show" the audience its moral duty or the actions (sometimes the identity) of the dramatis personae.

In a so-called Conversion or Saints' play, *The Conversion of St. Paul*, from the Digby manuscript probably composed originally in East Midland dialect of the late fifteenth century, soliloquy may be seen in a format possibly unique within medieval staging. The play, a mixture of Biblical materials and fable, is performed in three divisions at three separate "Stations." Each of the three Stations is introduced, and subsequently concluded, by "the poet," speaking a prologue and an epilogue to each division, "alone" on stage each time, using the seven-line *ababbcc* stanza of rime royal. Such procedure would seem to define anew the lines between "stage" and audience. But those lines are as intentionally blurred by other features of this play as though in a work by Brecht, in that the audience, after having marched in a procession as a congregation, must listen to a soliloquy-sermon by Saul, on the Seven Deadly Sins. In effect, the production becomes an act of worship, in which the author placed considerable structural dependence on soliloquy as, too, on the rime royal stanza. Another soliloquy, a routine vaunt by Belial, occurs midway in the action.

The Wakefield *Noah* contains a speech exemplifying the main structural factors of mystery soliloquy. Like the *Second Shepherds' Play*, this drama combines the comic and the lofty: Noah's *Uxor*, stubborn and willful, is quite reminiscent of Gyll, wife of the comic Mak, but the tale itself undoubtedly impressed its fifteenth-century audiences with a serious sense of reality concerning God's omnipotence and mercifulness, since a Noah pageant existed also in the York and Chester cycles.

As to the specific soliloquy in question, the *Noah* opens with a long rhymed speech by the title character. In the opening thirteen lines and in the closing nine, all of which hail deity in the second person, Noah is apparently speaking directly to the persona named "God." But Noah is speaking to the assembly in soliloquy about his God in the other fifty lines of the speech. They are phrased as a prayer-narrative, full of praises of the Lord as well as recitations of the story of the Fall and of the subsequent need for Noah's peculiar services as shipwright-savior. Only a few representative lines (from the central fifty) follow:

>   . . . Yit was ther unkindnes
>   More by foldys seven then I can well expres,
>   Forwhy
>   Of all angels in brightnes
>   God gaf Lucifer most lightnes,
>   Yit prowdly he flit his des

>   And set him even Him by.
>
>   He thoght himself as worthy as Him that him made
>   In brightnes, in bewty; therfor He him degrade,
>   Put him in a low degré soyn after, in a brade,
>   Him and all his menye, wher he may be unglad
>   For ever.
>   Shall thay never win away
>   Hence unto domysday,
>   Bot burn in bayle for ay;
>   Shall thay never dissever.
>   Soyne after, that gracious Lord to his liknes maide man,
>   That place to be restord, even as he began.
>   Of the Trinité by accord, Adam, and Eve that woman,
>   To multiplye without discord, in paradise put he thaym,
>   And sithen to both
>   Gaf in commaund
>   On the tre of life to lay no hend.
>   Bot yit the fals feynd
>   Made Him with man wroth, (11. 12-36)[19]

Noah's soliloquy defies exact definition. Although of homiletic tone, this long narrative serves also as a prologue to the play, summing up the story of mankind from Eden to the stage-present time, just prior to the Flood. The indefinableness can perhaps be most adequately expressed by saying, as Vincent F. Hopper and Gerald B. Lahey do in their Introduction to *Medieval Mysteries, Moralities, and Interludes* (Great Neck, N.Y.: 1962), p. 26: "Thus . . . the old lines of the ancient ritual drama of the folk run into and blend with the more conscious drama of art." The ritual of the earliest tropes supplies the direct ancestry of prayer-narratives such as Noah's, and the "more conscious drama of art" governs its simple-narrative aspects. One of the outstanding textual qualities of mystery soliloquy, and of most morality soliloquies as well, is seen in Noah's address, that is, the naiveté of language mentioned earlier in this chapter. The speech shows unquestioning acceptance of the Creation story from Genesis and is full of such phrases as "burn in hell" and "the false fiend," now commonly considered archaic and quaint. However, as Robert Heilman wisely cautions in his Introduction to *An Anthology of English Drama Before Shakespeare* (New York: 1952), pp. v-vi, such naiveté reflects an inevitable coercion on writers transcribing for a popular audience myths closely defined in documentary form, inherent circumscriptions of the artists' independence of composition.

Another speech of Noah, a very short one in lines 184-89 of the play, presents a combination of types of mystery soliloquy:

>   And I am agast that we get som fray
>   Betwixt us both.

> For she is full tethee,
> For litill oft angré;
> If any thing wrang be,
> Soyne is she wroth.

This little soliloquy by Noah, sandwiched between the exiting of God and the entry of Noah's wife, contains rudiments of character-soliloquy, since it sheds light on the husbandly apprehensions of the speaker as well as on his wife's capacity for testiness. But it is doubtless most conveniently, if not at all exclusively, classifiable as plot-action soliloquy in that it anticipates or predicts actions to come. Humorously, by their immediate juxtaposition to the above speech Noah's next words serve better to "characterize" him:

> God spede, dere wife! How fayre ye?

To sum up, soliloquy existed in the mysteries, as in all other epochs of drama, exclusively to inform the audience. With rare exceptions, it is couched in what is (aside from its customary rhyming) by far its most prominent textual characteristic, naiveté. It is dominated by plot-exposition and homily, the former disclosing either plot-action or role-action, the homily hardly ever found except in combination with the exposition. In its earliest centuries of importance, shortly after the new, medieval beginnings of drama in Europe, English mystery soliloquy acquired several new conventions. The thirteenth and fourteenth centuries begat, if in limited numbers, the monarch's command-to-quiet prologue, the sermon-exposition, the Satan-vaunt, the Mary and Joseph contemplations, and the parade of prophets. The fifteenth century brought forth many poignant prayer-soliloquies for the role of Jesus, and occasional introspections for that of Peter. It also spread wide the Herod-rant born two centuries previous, and, in farcical frame, elicited out of speaker-identifications the rudiments of character-revelation soliloquy, ever so lightly foreshadowing Hamlets and Macbeths to come.

Notes

Chapter II

[1] Joseph S. Tunison, *Dramatic Traditions of the Dark Ages* (Chicago: 1907), pp. 10-11.

[2] Tunison, pp. 10-11.

[3] Tunison, pp. 67-68.

[4] Introduction to *Seneca, His Tenne Tragedies Translated into English*, ed. Thos. Newton (1581; rpt. Bloomington, Ind.: n.d.), p. xxxvii.

[5] Richard Axton, *European Drama of the Middle Ages* (Pittsburgh: 1975), p. 133.

[6] *Non-Cycle Plays and Fragments*, ed. Norman Davis (London: 1970), pp. 114-15.

[7] Davis, p. 93.

[8] Davis, p. 106.

[9] E. K. Chambers, *The Mediaeval Stage* (Oxford: 1903), II, 70-71, says, "Most things about the *Adam* are in dispute."

[10] David Bevington, *Medieval Drama* (Boston: 1975), p. 113, n. 744.

[11] Bevington, pp. 113-14.

[12] Bevington, p. 268.

[13] Bevington is the source for the York, Wakefield, and N Town plays alluded to in these 3 pages but not quoted at length, as well as *The Conversion of St. Paul,* mentioned later in the chapter.

[14] Bevington, p. 515.

[15] Bevington, p. 527.

[16] Bevington, pp. 450-51.

[17] Quotations from *The Second Shepherds' Play* are from Bevington, p. 384ff.

[18] Davis, pp. 56-57.

[19] Quotations from the Wakefield *Noah* are from Bevington, p. 291ff.

Chapter III

Morality Drama

Three periods of morality drama are identified in this chapter. The first, to be termed Early Moralities, extends from approximately 1390 to 1500. The second, Intermediate Moralities, occupies the years from 1501 to the accession of Elizabeth in 1558. The third period, the years from 1559 to about 1585, represents the Late Moralities, often quite successful dramaturgically. Importantly, the main elements of morality soliloquy very often, though not irrefutably, continue conspicuously as more polished practices in Elizabethan soliloquy. Various terms such as doctrinal or propagandistic are used here from time to time to describe particular plays, but the regular basis, the most convenient, for classifying moralities is chronological. Because of the need to examinne distinctions in scope and given the vast number of structural variations in the two centuries of moralities, it becomes also necessary to particularize as to content and structure. The latter, because of its much greater variety, requires the lengthier treatment. This will be given last in the chapter.

As to the content of morality soliloquies, far and away the most notable conntributive element is the *debat* over the soul of mankind between allegorically named personifications of abstract virtues and vices. This psychomachic struggle between beneficent forces such as Perseverance and Reason and representatives of iniquity such as Sensuality and Avarice is also discussed throughout this chapter as a structural aspect. It dominates the stage in morality drama. But moral dicta to the audience represent only one of the two fundamental ingredients in morality soliloquy. The other, as in mystery drama, is exposition of plot, divisible into two sorts, over-all plot action and action by the soliloquy-speaker. Again as in mystery plays, each morality soliloquy generally communicates some combination of audience-information, rather than merely one kind.

The following soliloquy is typical of such combinings. It is uttered by Reason, in an early morality entitled *Nature*, written by Henry Medwall c. 1490-1501. Reason is vying with other allegorically named personae in a debate for control of Man. Sensuality, Pride and Worldly Affection have just gone offstage and Reason has come on:

> O good Lord! to whom shall I complain

> And show the sorrows of my mind?
> And nothing for mine own cause, certain;
> But only for the decay of mankind;
> Which now, of late, is waxen so blind
> That he hath despised and forsaken me,
> And followeth every motion of his Sensuality.
>   What availed at the beginning
> That Nature committed me to his service?
> And charged me that, before all thing,
> Of all his guiding I should take th' enterprise
> When he lusteth not to follow mine advice,
> But followeth th' appetites of his sensual affection,
> As a brute beast that lacketh reason?
>   And yet, notwithstanding
> That he doth me disdain,
> I will resort to him again;
> And do my labour and busy pain
> To assay if I can him refrain
> From such beastly living.
> But, first will I stand hereby,
> In secret manner, to espy
> Some token of grace in him, whereby
> I may discern and find
> That he hath any shamefacedness
> After his great surfeit and excess;
> And, if it be so, doubtless,
> It shall content my mind. (Part the First)[1]

Elements of plot-action soliloquy are visible within the first few lines:

> Which [mankind] now, of late, is waxen so blind
> That he hath despised and forsaken me,
> And followeth every motion of his Sensuality.

In this brief summary of the activities of the persona called Man, he is seen as despising and rejecting the persona named Reason. A component of role-action soliloquy is also present, in that Reason is describing his physical role as a persona in the drama ("Nature . . . charged me that . . . I should take th' enterprise"). At the same time he is speaking as a symbolic force for man's good. Roughly the first half of the piece is in allegorical language: Man has rejected Reason in favor of Sensuality. The final fourteen lines of the speech are another role-action disclosure by Reason, who is informing the audience as to just how he will now restrain Man from his excesses ("I will resort to him again"). But at the same time these concluding lines, even though mostly defining personal physical action ("I stand hereby,/ In secret manner, to espy"), are an integral part of the homiletic exposition which is the basic purpose of the speech and of the play. Taken as a whole, this soliloquy is a discourse of Reason deploring the fact that man blindly "followeth th' appetites of his sensual affection," and it illustrates the primary feature of morality soliloquy, the dramatization of moral allegory.

From this point on in the chapter, morality soliloquy will generally be sampled within a chronological ordering of plays. But before leaving the play *Nature*, here placed out of chronology because it so richly typifies morality soliloquies, one of its four other soliloquies, a tiny one spoken by Envy, may be noted as example of role-action declamation, describing or predicting the physical action of the speaker. Envy speaks:

> Alas! that I had no good fellow here
> To bear me company, and laugh at this gear:
> This game was well found. (Part the Second)

As the plot unfolds in ensuing lines, Envy's little speech operates as a plot-link to herald the entry of Sensuality, the next persona to appear, as well as a forecast of Envy's subsequent action, which is to "laugh at this gear" in company of some "good fellow" (Sensuality). If the soliloquy contains the barest implications of Envy's character, they remain to be defined in Sensuality's succeeding words, ". . . ye lust to play the knave," so the audience is not really informed about character within the soliloquy itself. Another speech, taken from what is described by Bevington in *From Mankind to Marlowe* (Cambr., Mass.: 1962), p. 48, as "the most indisputably popular play of the fifteenth century," further emphasizes that the two major components of morality soliloquy are homily and plot exposition. It is the early morality *Mankind* (c. 1470, during the reign of Edward IV). Mercy speaks:

> The very fownder & begynner of ower
>   fyrst creacion,
> A-monge ws synfull wrechys he oweth to be magnyfyede,
> That for ower dysobedyenc[e] he hade non indygnacion
> To sende hys own son to be torn & crucyfyede;
> Ower obsequyouse seruyce to hym xulde be aplyede;
> Where he was Lorde of all & made all thynge of nought,
> For the synfull synner to late hym revyuyde
> And for hys redempcyon sett hys own son at nought.
> That may be seyde & veryfyede: Mankynde was dere bought;
> By the pytouse deth of Ihesu he hade hys remedye;
> He was purgyde of hys defawte, that wrechydly hade
>   wrought,
> By hys gloryus Passyon, that blyssyde lauatorye.
> O souerence, I be-seche you yower condycyons to rectyfye
> Ande with hymylite & reuerence to haue a remocyon
> To this blyssyde prynce that ower nature doth gloryfye,
> That ye may be partycypable of hys retribucyon.
>
> I haue be the very mene for yower restytucyon;

Mercy ys my name, that mornyth for yower offence.
Dyverte not yower-sylffe in tyme of temtacyon,
That ye may be acceptable to Gode at yower goynge hence.
The grett Mercy of Gode, that ys of most pre-emmynence,
Be medyacyon [sic] of Ower Lady, that ys euer habundante
To the synfull creature that wyll repent hys ne[g]lygence, —
I prey Gode, at yower most nede that Mercy be yower
    defendawnte!

In goode werkys I a-wyse yow, souerence, to be perseuerante,
To puryfye yower sowlys that thei be not corupte;
For yower gostly enmy wyll make hys a-vaunte,
Yower goode condycions yf he may interupte.
O ȝe souerens that sytt, & ȝe brothern that stonde ryghte
    wppe,
Pryke not yower felycytes in thynges transytorye!
Be-holde not the erthe, but lyfte yower ey wppe!
Se how the hede the members dayly do magnyfye!
Who ys the hede, forsoth, I xall yow certyfye:
I mene ower Sauyower, that was lykynnyde to a lambe;
Ande hys sayntes be the members, that dayly he doth satysfye
With the precyose reuer that runnyth from hys wombe;
Ther ys non such foode by water ner by lande,
So precyouse, so gloryouse, so redefull to ower entent,
For yt hath dyssoluyde Mankynde from the bitter bonde
Of the mortall enmye, [the] venymouse serpente;

From the wyche Gode preserue yow all the last Iugement,
For sekyrly ther xall be a streat examynacyon;
The corn xall be sauyde, the chaffe xall be brente:
I be-sech yow hertyly, haue this premedytacyone. (11. 1-44)[2]

The entire speech is a mixture of sermon, role-action soliloquy, and prologue. The first sixteen lines are uninterruptedly sermon, memorializing Jesus' death for man's salvation and exhorting the audience to become worthy of that sacrifice (". . . he oweth to be/ magnyfyede"). Lines 17-24 combine homily and role-action speech: Mercy gives the audience his name, and informs them that he is the means of their restoration into God's favor ("That ye may be acceptable to Gode"). These lines are allegorical as well as depictive of persona-action — the audience may be restored to acceptability in God's sight through "the grett Mercy of Gode," which (Mercy) is both role-name and allegorical route to regeneration in the Christian faith. The remainder of Mercy's speech (11. 25-44) is mainly outright sermon, reminding the assembly of the never-ending war between good ("Gode") and evil ("venymouse serpents") for the soul of man. In entirety, this opening soliloquy in *Mankind* is in all but name also a prologue, since it reminds the audience of the general homiletic tone (if not the plot per se) of the play to come.

The personification of Death in the now best known of the moralities, *Everyman* (c. 1500), declaims a soliloquy on his initial entry into the play which serves as, in the words of Wolfgang Clemen in *English Tragedy Before Shakespeare*, trans. T. S. Dorsch (London: 1961), p. 115, "the 'self-introduction' and 'self-explanation' that were regularly employed as a dramatic convention on the first entry of the characters or personified abstractions in the Miracle and Morality plays." Death speaks to the audience as follows:

> Every man will I beset that liveth beastly
> Out of God's laws, and dreadeth not folly.
> He that loveth riches I will strike with my dart,
> His sight to blind, and from heaven to depart,
> Except that alms be his good friend,
> In hell for to dwell, world without end.
> Lo, yonder I see Everyman walking;
> Full little he thinketh on my coming;
> His mind is on fleshly lusts and his treasure;
> And great pain it shall cause him to endure
> Before the Lord, Heaven King. (11. 72-84)[3]

Here Death is voicing the combination of role-action soliloquy and homily examined previously in *Nature* and *Mankind*, and pervasive throughout morality drama. Within the same words he tells what he will do and presents a homily containing the reasons for such action. Like practically all morality soliloquy, this speech is to be interpreted on two levels, action in the play and allegory. As persona in the action Death is announcing that he will beset Everyman severely; on the allegorical level, the speech is a thinly disguised sermon admonishing that every man who lives "out of God's laws" will be hard pressed to escape hell when confronted by death. The duality of participating in stage-action and simultaneously allegorizing it is, again, the major aspect in the content of morality soliloquy.

Differences in the subject matter are often visible in homilies of intermediate and late moralities, as compared to the earlier dramas, in that soliloquies of *debat* in early morality dramas tend to be concerned with purely eschatological questions, while in intermediate and late moralities diversions to concerns of secular morality, social issues, or politics begin to appear in the debate speeches. Such a diversion is evident, for example, in the soliloquy by Good Counsel in the intermediate morality *Lusty Juventus* (1547-53), cited again later in the chapter for innovations in form. Good Counsel says:

> O merciful Lord, who can cease to lament,
> Or keep his heart from continual mourning,
> To see how Youth is fallen from thy word and testament,

And wholly inclined to Abhominable Living?
He liveth nothing according to his professing;
But, alas! his life is to thy word['s] abusion,
Except thy great mercy, to his utter confusion.
O, where is now the godly conversation,
Which should be among the professors of thy word!
O, where may a man find now one faithful congregation,
That is not infected with dissension or discord?[4]

The main purpose of this speech is propaganda. Written during the reign of the boy king Edward the Sixth, the play is a thrust against the Romish Church meant to advance the Reformation promulgated by Edward's father, Henry VIII. Good Counsel is lamenting the grievous error of young people who have fallen into the ways of their fathers' religion. He is also deploring the disappearance of faithful congregations, brotherly love and the fruits of God's spirit, thus rambling from his ostensible allegorical topic of the excesses of youth gone over to "Abhominable [sic] Living." The speech is replete with righteous-sounding platitudes no doubt acceptable *en masse* to his audience accustomed to having the stage supplement the pulpit. But the main message of the allegory is not simply to live virtuously; virtue resides in adopting and continuing the new faith.

Whatever the topic, this sermonic soliloquy and all morality homilies reflect their original basis in the psychomachia, man's struggle between forces of good and evil. The above passages from typical moralities demonstrate the typical materials of morality soliloquy: homily (in its various forms, the primary one being allegorical debate), and plot exposition (of over-all plot action or of role action). More often than not a given soliloquy contains elements from both these major areas, a fact true also of mystery soliloquies earlier and of Shakespearean soliloquies later.

The forms of morality soliloquy show many differences from soliloquy in earlier religious drama. First of all, the delivering agent has evolved. Instead of Bible figure, he is now allegorical abstraction. In place of Abraham or Noah now are heard Everyman or Perseverance, and Belial or Mischief rather than Judas. Evil is still opposed to Good, but now they are both called by their own names, as it were, often giving soliloquy a dual burden, as observed previously, of explaining both the role of the speaker and its significance in the plot (or in life itself). The characters focus and react on one another, even though they may be abstractions instead of earthly beings. Mankind is the morally educable person and Goodness, Perseverance, the Seven Deadly Sins, and even Death are all portrayed as attempting to take charge of his education. But the result is allegory, not naturalistic characterization, because virtually all important morality soliloquies exist within and for the purpose of the debate between Good and Evil. Whatever the names for Good and Evil: Perseverance, Good Counsel, Mischief, Crafty Conveyance, the all-pervasive emphasis is on the psychomachia for the control of man's soul. This debate is far and away the most distinctive aspect of structure in morality soliloquies, as it is also the chief contributive factor to their homiletic component.

However, marked deviations in form, as in content, exist between soliloquies in early moralities and those in intermediate and late moralities. To name only a few, particular divergencies are found in types of names given to personified abstractions, in language, and in poetic technique, all yet to be reviewed in this chapter. The over-all dissimilarities, however, are in greatly increased literary sophistication and heightened sense of dramatization seen (with glaring exceptions, noted below) in soliloquies from intermediate and late moralities. In short, in the early plays soliloquy form is by no means so varied as that in intermediate and late plays, with the Herod-rant of the mysteries — now become an alliterating Vice-vaunt — the characteristic soliloquy in the early plays. With this in mind, and in view of the fact that soliloquy form in the later plays has much more in common with, and evolutionary effect on, structure in Shakespearean soliloquies, one specimen typical of early morality soliloquy should suffice for examination in this section, where the major emphasis will be on aspects of structure in several speeches from intermediate and late moralities.

The specimen from early morality soliloquy is the vaunt of Belial in *The Castle of Perseverance*.[5] Only a few representative lines of the vaunt are reproduced here; the speech will be cited in the following chapter for other purposes. Belial proclaims:

> Now I sit, Satanas, in my sad sin,
> As devil doughty, in draff as a drake;
> . . . .
> What folk that I grope, they gapen and grin.
> Iwis, from Carlisle into Kent my carping they take.
> Both the back and the buttock bursteth all on brenne
> With works of wreche. I work them mickle wrake;
> In woe is all my wenne.[6]

As usual in early moralities, the tone of Belial's vaunt is that of a kind of open warfare between Belial and mankind in general, a military psychomachia. He is taunting his victims, intentionally and openly working them much woe. Belial is Vice itself, undisguised by the layers of literary polish likely in later morality plays. The insistent exactness of rhyme and the unremitting alliterativeness can only be described as primitive poetic technique. Elements of buffoonery and coarseness, seen frequently in early moralities, heighten the impression of primitiveness of technique, as in the bawdy acerbity of Belial's description of his victims as gaping and grinning, with buttocks aflame. Such lines must practically have forced the speaker to spit the words through his teeth in raspingly satiric tone, inducing the audience to laughter at something patently within their conventional concept of evil. In sum, both the action suggested by the soliloquy and the language describing that action are quite the usual sort to be encountered in early moralities, and are of course primitive by standards observed in most intermediate and late morality plays, standards reviewed in the pages ensuing.

Several of the structural tenets of soliloquy in intermediate and late moralities underly the speech by Counterfeit Countenance in Stage 2, Scene 8 of John Skelton's *Magnificence*. Even though this play (c. 1513-16) is an intermediate morality, its poetry is superior to that of most late moralities, the more remarkable when its chronological closeness to the eschatological moralities of the late fifteenth century is noted. In *Shakespeare and the Allegory of Evil* (New York: 1958), p. 215, Bernard Spivack appropriately calls *Magnificence* "the most literary and artistic of the allegorical plays." The speech is the second of seven soliloquies in what might be termed a series interspersed throughout the play, all of them identifying abstraction-personae as to allegorical significance in the debate for moral authority over the hero (Magnificence). The others in the series are spoken by Felicity, Cloakéd Collusion, Courtly Abusion, Fancy, Crafty Conveyance, and Liberty. (Speaking the initial soliloquy of the play, Felicity signifies the hard-to-win prize in this drama, patently a measure of Good.) Counterfeit Countenance speaks his soliloquy as follows:

> Fancy hath catchéd in a fly-net
> This noble man Magnificence,
> Of Largesse under the pretence.
> They have made me here to put the stone:
> But now will I, that they be gone,
> In bastard time, after the doggerel guise,
> Tell you whereof my name doth rise.
> For Counterfeit Countenance known am I,
> This world is full of my folly.
> I set not by him a fly
> That cannot counterfeit a lie,
> Swear, and stare, and bide thereby,
> And countenance it cleanly,
> And defend it mannerly.
> . . . .
> Counterfeit kindness, and think deceit;
> Counterfeit letters by the way of sleight;
> Subtily using counterfeit weight;
> Counterfeit language, *fait bon geyt*.
> Counterfeit is a proper bait;
> A count to counterfeit in a receipt, —
> To counterfeit well is a good conceit.
> . . . .

>Counterfeit preaching, and believe the contrary;
>Counterfeit conscience, peevish pope holy;
>Counterfeit sadness, with dealing full madly;
>Counterfeit holiness is calléd hypocrisy;
>Counterfeit reason is not worth a fly;
>Counterfeit wisdom, and works of folly;
>Counterfeit countenance every man doth occupy.
>. . . . .
>   (Stanzas 1, 2, 6, 10)[7]

Counterfeit Countenance, the delivering agent of this soliloquy, is obviously a personification of vice, but as usual in intermediate and late moralities he is one of several vices in the play who share virtually equal importance in the struggle to corrupt the hero. His soliloquy announces one kind of vice which the prince of the realm (here doubtless the real intended "audience") must avoid if he is to enjoy order and felicity in his reign. This speech (like those of his fellows, Courtly Abusion, Liberty, Fancy, etc.) displays a persona boasting of prowess in his chosen area of mischief-making, and, at the same time, homilizing as to the dangers inherent in following his precepts. In these respects this vaunt by Counterfeit Countenance is very much like the vaunts of the devils in the warfare psychomachia of the earliest moralities. However, when in intermediate and late allegories mankind came to signify a being capable of emotion and no longer merely a generic term for the focal point of psychomachic battles, the vices in moralities were awarded names of allegorical qualities rather than of Christianity's devils or Deadly Sins, and their vaunts came to resemble boastings of egocentric human figures as much as harangues of evil intent. This heightening from simple demon-figure to rudimentary characterization is readily apparent in the soliloquies of the vices in *Magnificence*.

The language of the above soliloquy exemplifies the best found in intermediate or late dramas, despite, as mentioned before, the rather early date of the play. Gone is most of the coarseness and buffoonery often remarked in earlier moralities; the diction of Counterfeit Countenance is much more polished than that of Belial cited above from *Castle of Perseverance*. Alliteration, for instance, while noticeable throughout the speech, is much less insistent than in the earlier tradition (other than in the allegorical naming of this vice). It is barely present in the first stanza, more visible in the second: "*f*ull of my *f*olly," "*c*annot *c*ounterfeit," "*S*wear, and *s*tare". Alliterative repetition at line-beginnings frequently appears, of course, as in the final two stanzas quoted, dinning the speaker's name into audience consciousness. This line-opening repetition also helps cloak portions in a rollicking rhythm probably never found in early morality soliloquy, a rhythm produced by Skelton's technique of following the dactyl "*Coun*terfeit" with other dactyls or with trochees ("*Coun*terfeit *preach*ing, and" "*Coun*terfeit *con*science, *pee*vish"). Another mark of relative sophistication lies in the word-play of the penultimate quoted stanza, isolated instance though it may be, where in the final two lines the poet echoes the syllable "count" in two other words, "counterfeit" and "conceit" (initial syllable).

Much more obvious resemblance to vaunts from the earlier dramas appears in a soliloquy by Cloakéd Collusion a bit later in *Magnificence* (Stage 2, Scene 11), another in the series of allegorical-significance soliloquies delivered by the vices. The stage-directions for the speech state, "Here CLOAKÉD COLLUSION promenades." A few lines (the second stanza) demonstrate the nature of the speech:

> Double dealing and I be all one,
>   Crafting and hafting contrivéd is by me;
> I can dissemble, I can both laugh and groan,
>   Plain dealing and I can never agree:
>   But divísion, dissensíon, derisíon, these three
> And I am counterfeit of one minde and thought,
> By the means of mischief to bring all thinge to nought.[8]

One can picture Cloakéd Collusion strutting at forestage in this throwback to the earlier tradition of vaunt, appearing to be

> devisinge the meanes and ways that I can,
> How I may hurte and hinder every man.

In the soliloquy quoted just prior to this one, Counterfeit Countenance is frequently placed in the role of describing as an abstraction the concept of vice he represents, of speaking of Counterfeit as a quality or a universal activity. But here Cloakéd Collusion speaks almost entirely in the first person, describing his own odious actions past and present, more like the vice in an early morality.

Two other soliloquies in *Magnificence* demand attention here as to distinctiveness of form. The title character, Magnificence, speaks both of them, and both fall under the category of lament soliloquy analyzed at length in Chapter v. The first speech, from Stage 4, Scene 28, is preceded by stage-directions bearing on its form. It follows:

> Here MAGNIFICENCE dolorously makes his moan
> O feeble fortune, O doleful destiny!
> O hateful hap, O careful cruelty!
> O sighing sorrow, O thoughtful misery!
> O redeless ruth, O painful poverty!
> O dolorous heart, O hard adversity!
> O odious distress, O deadly pain and woe!
> For worldy [sic] shame I wax both wan and blo.
>
> Where is now my wealth and my noble estate?

> Where is now my treasure, my lands, and my rent?
> Where is now all my servants that I had here of late?
> Where is now my gold upon them that I spent?
> Where is now all my rich habiliment?
> Where is now my kin, my friends, and my noble blood?
> Where is now all my pleasure and my worldy [sic] good?
>
> Alas, my folly! alas, my wanton will!
> I may no more speak, till I have wept my fill.[9]

This soliloquy exemplifies the apostrophe to grief or woe described by Wolfgang Clemen in Chapter xiv of *English Tragedy Before Shakespeare*, an entire chapter devoted to the Dramatic Lament in its various forms. In a sense, especially in the seventh line ("I wax both wan and blo") and in the final couplet ("till I have wept my fill"), the persona named Magnificence is formally announcing to the audience his own emotive nature, comparably to the manner in which personae delivering role-action soliloquies announce their own stage-actions. As to language, the formulaic repetition of "O" is of course inescapable. But the alliteration in the initial seven lines, so primitive looking at first reading, seems on re-examination rather carefully achieved. While seven instances of adjective-noun alliteration do occur in those seven lines ("*f*eeble *f*ortune," "*d*oleful *d*estiny," etc.), the other five expressions of woeful fortune in those lines ("*t*houghtful *m*isery," "*d*olorous *h*eart," etc.) do not alliterate. In the remainder of the lament, "Where" and "now" repeat continuously, but alliteration within lines is not nearly so common ("*W*here . . . *w*ealth" and "*w*anton *w*ill").

The second lament by the hero Magnificence occurs at the end of Stage 4, Scene 29:

> Alas, mine own servants to shew me such reproach,
> Thus to rebuke me, and have me in despite!
> So shamefully to me, their master, to approach,
> That sometime was a noble prince of might!
> Alas, to live longer I have no delight!
> For to live in misery it is harder than death.
> I am weary of the world, for unkindness me slèeth.[10]

This brief soliloquy serves more than one function. In its first four lines it reminds the audience of the immediate past action of the plot and forms a link between scenes of the play. In its other three lines ("to live longer I have no delight!") it bears a resemblance to the form described by Professor Clemen as the prayer for annihilation, (p. 243) although it might more accurately be noted as exemplifying *contemptus mundi*, since the persona's demise is not apostrophized or asked for directly. In language this speech is much more sophisticated than the previous lament by Magnificence, quite subtly employing alliteration, for example, as in "*s*ervants to *s*hew," "*m*e, their *m*aster," and "*l*ive longer . . . de*l*ight." In fact, the speech compares favorably with passages in plays written much later.

A speech by Envy in *Impatient Poverty* (Anon., 1547-48) illuminates structural factors of most soliloquies in intermediate moralities, although it does not contain as many separate techniques as the first soliloquy by Counterfeit Countenance quoted above from *Magnificence*. Envy speaks:

> Is he gone? then have at laughing!
> A, sir! is not this a jolly game
> That Conscience doth not know my name?
> Envy, in faith! I am the same:
> What needeth me for to lie?
> I hate Conscience, Peace, Love and Rest;
> Debate and Strife, that love I best,
> According to my property.
> When a man loveth well his wife,
> I bring them at debate and strife —
> This is seen daily;
> Also, between sister and brother;
> There shall no neighbour love another
> Where I dwell by.
> And now I tell you plain,
> Of one man I have disdain;
> Prosperity men do him call.
> He is nigh of my blood;
> And he to have so much worldly good,
> That grieveth me worst of all.[11]

The speech begins somewhat unusually; in place of the stage-direction "Exit" Envy's own words show the departure of Conscience, whom he has just sent away "into some far country." After five lines spoken to Conscience, Envy asks, "Is he gone?" and then commences, alone on stage, to address the assemblage. Like Skelton's play, *Impatient Poverty* is primarily concerned with secular morality, rather than with eschatological themes; only an occasional line in the play gives lip service to the older Heaven and Hell warfare. The main purpose of the play is to advise the audience on the virtues which advance, or the vices which prevent, the gaining of riches. In fact, the hero's name changes during the course of events from Poverty to Prosperity, indicating that he has learned such lessons well. Envy is the Vice of this play. His allegorical name suggests overt evil; he represents one of the Seven Cardinal Sins. The speech is a vaunt, similar to the ones from *Magnificence* described earlier. In boastful laughter ("then have at laughing!") Envy identifies himself, describes his jolly game of sowing discord among families and neighbors, and aims his scorn directly at Prosperity. The function of Envy here is virtually that of director of the play, narrating how the action shall proceed. The language of this soliloquy, containing many iambics, is more colloquial than that of Skelton's allegorical figures, but rather less rewarding as poetry. Its rhyming is highly noticeable in its exactness, and in this respect fairly close to that of early moralities. The few alliterations in the speech appear incidental ("loveth *well* his *wife*," "*he* to *have*"). The soliloquy of Envy better represents typical form than commendable artistry in intermediate morality soliloquy.

A very short space beyond in the play, Envy has another soliloquy, practically identical in form and function. Prosperity departs for "some recreation," and after bidding him bon voyage, in the prefatory couplet, Envy shares with the audience his conspiratorial laughter and purpose regarding the hero:

> He that sitteth above the moon
> Evermore be in your protection!
> Aha! here is sport for a lord,
> That Prosperity and I be well at accord!
> I shall bring his thrift under the board,
> I trust, within short space.
> For it grieveth my heart right sore
> He hath so much treasure in store,
> And I have never the more.
> I must find some proper shift
> That from his good he may be lift;
> To bring him to Misrule I hold it best,
> For he can soon bring it to pass.

Peace, an allegorical representation of an attainable Good, delivers a bit later on what amounts in substance to a direct opposite of the vaunts of Envy:

> When Phebus draweth into the occidental,
> And obscured with clouds misty and dark,
> Then trees, herbs, and grass, by course natural,
> Want their chief comfort: thus saith many a clerk.
> And, likewise, that a man in his wark
> Is destitute of reason following sensual operation.
> The last time I was in this place
> Prosperity unto Misrule put his whole confidence.
> He regarded not my counsel; he lacked grace;
> Which, in time coming, shall turn him to inconvenience.
> With hazarders and rioters he keepeth residence
> At clash and cards, with all unthrifty game;
> Which, in continuance, shall bring him shame.
> To him yet I will resort:
> If he be brought in poverty
> I shall do him all the comfort

> And all the help that lieth in me;
> I will never rest till I him see.
> But seek about, from place to place,
> And bring him to some better grace.

In physical form this of course hardly differs from the soliloquies quoted from Envy. After several lines deploring man's frequent succumbing to "sensual operation," Peace utters to the hearers *his* purpose ("some better grace") for the hero. But the purpose of Peace, and the tone of his utterance, are benevolent: Peace is not laughing at Prosperity, but simply reporting rather restrainedly on his excesses. The speech also serves as plot link between the exit of Envy and Prosperity, who have departed together, and the entry of Misrule immediately following the soliloquy by Peace.

Poverty (Prosperity) speaks a brief lament soliloquy a few pages farther on:

> O Jesu! what may this mean?
> My goods are spent and wasted away!
> Also my men are from me clean;
> I see them not this seven nights' day.
> As long as I might spend and pay,
> They held me up with false dissimulation;
> And now they forsake me in my most tribulation.

The content of this speech, primarily plot-action summary, may well be more important to the play than its lament form, but the speech typifies the latter, so often found in moralities. A much longer lament by the same persona occurs just a few lines farther on in the scene. Envy, in the guise of Charity, has just left, and Poverty speaks again:

> Abide still with me, gentle Charity!
> O, to whom should I sue, to whom should I plette?
> O mortal worm, wrapped all in woe!
> As a man all mortified, and mased in my wit,
> I, a captive in captivity, lo, fortune is my foe!
> I am in endless sorrow; alas! what shall I do?
> These caitiffs, through their counsel and false imagination,
> Have brought me to nought that was of great reputation.
> Woe worth the time that I them knew!
> I may well sigh, and say Alas!
> For now I find these words full true
> That Peace showed me here in this place.
> I regarded not his counsel; I lacked grace;
> Wherefore needy poverty on me doth blow his horn,
> That every man and woman doth laugh me to scorn.
> Example to all young men, when they take in hand
> To occupy in the world: for your behoof

> Look wisely before, and also understand
> Evil company destroyeth man — on me ye see the proof.
> Make a sure foundation or ye set up the roof.
> Of a good and virtuous beginning cometh a good ending;
> And evermore beware of unmeasurable spending!

The soliloquy begins with a lament to woe, but in its closing lines turns into homily, less an exhortation to moral virtue than to "beware of unmeasurable spending!"

Lusty Juventus, written by one R. Wever during the reign of Edward the Sixth (1547-53), contains five soliloquies, and at least one of them introduces an element not hitherto noted in this study of soliloquy in intermediate and late moralities, but earlier remarked occasionally in mystery drama: in the Prologue of the Messenger, chapter and verse of Scripture are formally quoted, very nearly verbatim. A brief passage showing the Scriptural quotations follows:

> For as much as man is naturally prone
> To evil from his youth, as Scripture doth recite,
> It is necessary that he be speedily withdrawn
> From concupiscence of sin, his natural appetite:
> An order to bring up youth Ecclesiasticus doth write, —
> An untamed horse will be hard, saith he,
> And a wanton child wilful will be.
>   Give him no liberty in youth, nor his folly excuse,
> Bow down his neck, and keep him in good awe,
> Lest he be stubborn: no labour refuse
> To train him to wisdom and teach him God's law,
> For youth is frail and easy to draw
> By grace to goodness, by nature to ill:
> That nature hath ingrafted, is hard to kill.[12]

This portion of the speech is meant as a sermon, opening a play designed (as explained earlier in this chapter) to combat the superstitions of the Romish Church and thus to advance the Reformation; the Messenger is not seen elsewhere in the play. The first two lines reflect both Genesis viii.21 and Jeremiah xvii.9:

> . . . for the imagination of man's heart is evil from his youth. (Gen. viii.21)
>
> The heart is deceitful above all things, and desperately wicked: who can know it? (Jer. xvii.9)[13]

And in the Apocryphal book of Ecclesiasticus, xxx.8, the reference given in lines 6 and 7 of the Messenger's speech reads:

> An horse not broken becometh headstrong: and a child left to

himself will be wilful.[14]

Beyond the fact of sermonic citation of Bible verses, the speech serves in its final half as traditional prologue to the action of the morality.

Satan the Devil speaks in soliloquy later in the piece:

> O, O, all too late!
> I trow this gear will come to naught;
> For I perceive my power doth abate,
> For all the policy that ever I have wrought:
> Many and sundry ways I have fought,
> To have the Word of God deluded utterly;
> O for sorrow! yet it will not be.
> I have done the best that I can,
> And my mistress also in every place,
> To root it clean from the heart of man;
> And yet for all that it flourisheth apace;
> I am sore in dread to show my face,
> My auctority and works are so greatly despised,
> My inventions, and all that ever I have devised.
> O, O, full well I know the cause,
> That my estimation doth thus decay;
> The old people would believe still in my laws,
> But the younger sort lead them a contrary way;
> They will not believe, they plainly say,
> In old traditions and made by men,
> But they will live, as the Scripture teacheth them.
> . . . . [15]

Satan is not the Vice of the play, nor is his speech a vaunt. If anything, this Satan is cast not as a villain but as an ineffectual bumbler almost eliciting sympathy from the play-viewers. Nothing he has done seems to have come right ("I trow this gear will come to naught"). Indeed, he is allegorically lamenting the passing of his stock in trade, Romish superstition, and that young people nowadays are mostly friends to the Reformation.

Hypocrisy is the Vice of this drama. His soliloquy, a little farther on, does exemplify the vaunt format seen in the other moralities quoted in this section:

> I warrant you, let me alone.
> I will be with Juventus anon,
> And that, ere he be ware;
> And, i-wis, if he walk not straight,
> I will use such a sleight,
> That shall trap him in a snare.
> How shall I bring this gear to pass?

> I can tell now, by the mass,
> Without any more advisement:
> I will infect him with wicked company,
> Whose conversation shall be so fleshly,
> Yea, able to overcome an innocent.
> This wicked Fellowship
> Shall him company keep
> For a while:
> And then I will bring in
> Abhominable Living,
> Him to beguile.
> With words fair I will him 'tice,
> Telling him of a girl nice,
> Which shall him somewhat move;
> Abhominable Living though she be,
> Yet he shall no other ways see,
> But she is for to love.
> . . . .[16]

Hypocrisy's tone of ultra-clever confidentiality is the same as that of Counterfeit Countenance in *Magnificence* and all the other representatives of vice cited in this chapter. But his method is rather the reverse of most such figures. First he struttingly shares with the audience the details of the stratagem he will perpetrate on Juventus, and then he identifies himself as to allegorical name and function.

Intermediate and late moralities generally contain at least one soliloquy of lament. Good Counsel speaks one in *Lusty Juventus*, excerpted earlier in the chapter as example of content:

> O merciful Lord, who can cease to lament,
> Or keep his heart from continual mourning,
> To see how Youth is fallen from thy word and testament,
> And wholly inclined to Abhominable Living?
> He liveth nothing according to his professing;
> But, alas! his life is to thy word['s] abusion,
> Except thy great mercy, to his utter confusion.
>
> . . . .
>
> O, what a joyful sight was it for to see,
> When Youth began God's word to embrace?
> Then he promised Godly Knowledge and me,
> That from our instruction he would never turn his face;
> But now he walketh, alas! in the ungodly's chase!
> Heaping sin upon sin, vice upon vice:[17]

Good Counsel's lament on the errors of youth is of course meant to be taken on two levels. As to plot-action, Youth has been attracted to the unwholesome female Abhominable Living; on the allegorical level, young people nowadays are to be lamented as fallen into the grievous error of return to their fathers' Papism. The author does not include quite so many "O's" as does Skelton when Magnificence "dolorously makes his moan" earlier in this chapter (twelve "O's" for Skelton), but enough of them occur to prevent the audience from mistaking the main purpose of the speech as anything but lament. (There are seven "O's.")

A word as to relative physical location of speaker and audience is pertinent here. Moralities were usually performed in an open space, called the "place," or on platforms named "mansions." Physically, the actor was quite close to his hearers. He was surrounded by them on three sides, or sometimes four (in *Castle of Perseverance*, for example). Some of the people were only a few feet from him in the manner seen sometimes in crowded Elizabethan theatres, where groundlings might be pressing near the edges of the stage, or on occasion dandies might even be sitting on its boundaries. In the presentation of the moralities there was no formal division between stage and auditorium as in most present-day performances. Thus there was also much less distinction than now between the world of the play and the real world of the audience, and in view of the permanent, non-mobile structure of Elizabethan theatres much less such distinction than in Shakespeare's era, too. When Satan exults in his victory over Worldly Man near the end of the late morality *Enough Is as Good as a Feast* (c. 1560-70, by W. Wager), his sermon — for it is one, despite the identity of the speaker — is not only addressed to the audience in the general sense of a theatre crowd but is also addressed particularly to the "worldly men" within the specific group in front of the speaker at a specific performance. A few of the forty-four lines of the speech by Satan, the concluding example of form from morality soliloquy, suffice to show this intimacy of address. Although this soliloquy may be described as a vaunt, Satan is not the Vice in this drama. That role is filled principally by Covetousness among three other figures of vice, Temerity, Inconsideration, and Precipitation. Satan speaks:

> Oh, oh, oh, oh! All is mine, all is mine!
> My kingdom increaseth every hour and day.
> Oh, how they seek my majesty divine!
> To come to me, they labor all that they may.
> . . . .
> All you worldly men, that in your riches do trust,
> Be merry and jocund, build palaces and make lusty cheer;
> Put your money to usury, let it not lie and rust;
> Occupy yourselves in my laws while ye be here.
> Spare not nor care not what mischief you frequent;
> Use drunkenness, deceit, take other men's wives;
> Pass of nothing — one hour is enough to repent

Of all the wickedness you have done in your lives.
Oh, if you will thus after my laws behave,
You shall have all things, as this Worldly Man had.
. . . .
Yea, and after death I will provide a place
For you in my kingdom forever to reign.
You shall fare no worse than doth mine own grace —
That is, to lie burning forever in pain.[18]

In the heavily ironic, tongue-in-cheek counsel given by Satan to the "worldly men" in the crowd in such lines as "one hour is enough to repent" and "I will provide a place/ For you in my kingdom" (a direct parody of Scripture), the audience is induced to laugh without at first realizing that their laughter is directed at their own weaknesses, at errors considered patently wrong by the society in which they live, usuriousness, drunkenness, deceit, adultery. Soliloquy in intermediate and late moralities often produces a kind of *théâtre intime* involving itself in the lives of the men and women in the assemblage, making them subject to and blameworthy for the errors of worldliness described homiletically by the speaker.

To summarize briefly, soliloquy structure differs very considerably between early moralities and intermediate/late moralities. The later periods show much more sophistication and variety in language, and a much greater sense of dramatization through soliloquy. Some of the praiseworthy differences include skillful alliteration, frequent intentional phrase-repetition, more specific stage-directions and a general progression from out of entirely allegorical representation of personae into character-portrayal more resembling Elizabethan modes (although still primarily allegorical and thus far more primitive than the Elizabethan). The principal vehicle for soliloquy in the later two periods is the vaunt, continued, with variances noted above, from the early moralities. Other main forms are soliloquies of prologue, lament, plot-link (always in combination with another form), and sermon per se. The primary formulaic aspect of morality soliloquies, early or late, however, is that of all eras in dramatic soliloquy, direct addressing of information to an audience.

It is an irrefutable fact that Elizabethan drama evolved directly out of its medieval English forebears. Schell and Shuchter remark in their Introduction to *English Morality Plays and Moral Interludes*, p. xxv: ". . . that period from the development of a popular English drama in the fourteenth century to the closing of the theatres in 1642 . . . is a time which might profitably be conceived as a single unbroken period of secularized religious drama whose central dramatic action involves the moral career of the Christian Mankind figure. Looked at from that point of view the mystery cycles, the moralities, and the Elizabethan plays can be thought of as different styles for the representation of a fundamentally unchanging subject matter."[19]

The medieval heritage of the Elizabethan stage, and of Shakespearean soliloquy, is perhaps more clearly traceable than anywhere else in medieval drama in a number of plays which can best be described as hybrid.[20] These have very much of the morality drama in them — indeed, some are generally classified as morality interludes — but they also evidence much breaking-away from the morality conventions. They exhibit both the stereotypings of the morality platform-stage and a new, heightened awareness of individualized characterization, offering both the depersonalized audience-addresses of medieval set speech and an occasional soliloquy revealing the personal feelings of a character. In short, as Willard Farnham says, the protagonist in these plays "tends to lose the abstract quality of *Humanum Genus*," portrayed throughout fifteenth-century drama.[21] Here is what Chambers (II, 149) called "that transformation of the medieval into the humanist type of drama, which prepared the way for the great Elizabethan stage."

Such a hybrid play from the late moralities is *Appius and Virginia* (licensed 1567, printed 1575). It is called by Farnham one of the three moralities of the 1560's which stand closest to the immediately pre-Shakespearean popular tragedy (the other two being *History of Horestes*, c. 1567, and *Cambises King of Persia*, c. 1569-70).[22] Appius, villain of this play, engages in a soliloquy late in the drama containing then-popular Senecan elements of repetitiveness, calculated formalism, and stichomythic dueling between abstraction-personae (e.g., Conscience vs. Justice). More importantly, the soliloquy reveals Appius to be at war within himself:

> But out I am wounded, how am I divided!
> Two states of my life from me are now glided;
> For Conscience he pricketh me contemned,
> And Justice saith, Judgement would have me condemned:
> Conscience saith, cruelty sure will detest me:
> And Justice saith, death in th' end will molest me:
> And both in one sudden me-thinks they do cry,
> That fire eternal, my soul shall destroy.
>
> (11. 501-08)[23]

Spivack remarks, p. 271, that this "in a cruder style, might be Angelo or Macbeth speaking, or Richard III debating with his conscience on the night before Bosworth. We have arrived, in short, at the Elizabethan soliloquy. The 'Holy War' externalized by the morality convention is now being restored to subjectivity as the divided voice within the hearts of individual men."

Another soliloquy in *Appius and Virginia* hearkens backward in time, rather than forward to Shakespeare's era. That is the speech of the Vice demonstrating (in the person of Haphazard) the limitless range of his influence in a genuinely medieval vaunt. Says Spivack: "What the Vice [Haphazard] cannot actually demonstrate to the audience he tells them about — his universal influence over all classes and occupations: courtiers, plowmen, merchants, scholars, schoolmasters, wives, and maids. All subscribe to the doctrine of haphazard fortune:

> Most of all these my nature doth injoy
> Somtime Iaduaunce them, somtime I destroy . . .
> (11. 222-23)"[24]

One more brief era needs to be examined in this review, namely, the works immediately prior to Shakespeare, the so-called transitional drama which dramaturgically, if not always chronologically, falls between the late morality plays and the Shakespearean. Two of its salient examples are Kyd's *Spanish Tragedy* (c. 1586) and Marlowe's *Faustus* (variously dated, but prob. 1592 or 1593, says Irving Ribner[25]).

The Spanish Tragedy is replete with set speeches; typical are the one uttered by Hieronimo to open Act III, Scene ii, and the one spoken by Lorenzo to close the same scene, in which orations Kyd thoroughly informs the audience concerning the two poles of force in the play. A composite of medieval and Elizabethan dramatic artifice, but with more of the latter's refinements than its immediate predecessors such as *Appius and Virginia*, the play does not feature a devil per se, as Marlowe's play does in plural, but it opens with a "Chorus" representing the Ghost of the Spanish courtier Andrea and his companion, Revenge. Revenge is a medieval abstraction-character; the ghost type appears later openly in several of Shakespeare's works, as Hamlet's father, Richard III's "conscience" just before Bosworth, and Macbeth's "vision," among others.

The two soliloquies reviewed here from Kyd's play well exemplify the content of transitional soliloquy (as of medieval soliloquy), that is, exposition of plot (of over-all plot action or of role action), and homily. The first speech, Hieronimo's, opens Act III, Scene ii:

> O eyes! no eyes, but fountains fraught with tears;
> O life! no life, but lively form of death;
> O world! no world, but mass of public wrongs,
> Confused and filled with murder and misdeeds!
> O sacred heavens! If this unhallowed deed,
> If this inhuman and barbarous attempt,
> If this incomparable murder thus
> Of mine, but now no more my son,
> Shall unrevealed and unrevenged pass,
> How should we term your dealings to be just,
> If you unjustly deal with those that in your justice trust?
> The night, sad secretary to my moans,

With direful visions wake my vexed soul,
And with the wounds of my distressful son
Solicit me for notice of his death.[26]

In this speech, nearly obscured by Senecan rhetorical device, is a combination of role-action exposition (Hieronimo's intent to avenge the death of his son), and homily (his justification for avenging his son's murder).

The soliloquy of Lorenzo closes the scene begun by Hieronimo's oration. Lorenzo says, to himself as it were:

And better it's that base companions die
Than by their life to hazard our good haps.
Nor shall they live, for me to fear their faith:
I'll trust myself, myself shall be my friend;
For die they shall, —
Slaves are ordained to no other end.[27]

This is both "self-addressed" homily and role-action exposition, homily in Lorenzo's opening justification for slaying base companions and role-action in his declaration that they shall die. It is not nearly so much rhetorically embellished as the speech by Hieronimo, if only because Lorenzo's purpose is much more mundane, to inform the assembly of a routine turn of plot rather than of a son's death requiring vengeance.

In form, the soliloquy of Hieronimo is a dramatic lament, representing the particular type that Clemen calls "the formal apostrophe to grief or woe," as in the string of apostrophes declaimed by the Nurse at Juliet's death (IV.v.9ff).[28] As to language in the soliloquy, bombast is the pejorative most often used for the Senecan soliloquy of pre-Shakespearean drama, as now and again for an early Shakespearean soliloquy. The great amount of apostrophe, contraries, high-charged adjectives and generally figurative language bequeathed to pre-Shakespearean soliloquy by Seneca is eminent in Hieronimo's utterance. The formal level of diction, the utter disregard for anything approaching vernacular or "realistic" language, the preciousness of the bisyllabic verbs (not of the monosyllable ones), the forced alliteration ("to *f*ear their *f*aith," "*f*ountains *f*raught"), and the over-all tone of declamation render the word "bombast" not inaccurately descriptive of this soliloquy by Kyd.

The opening line sets the Senecan tone pervading the segment, which is entirely representative of the complete speech. In the second line is a play on words ("no life, but lively"); in the third and fourth the venerable *contemptus mundi*. The heavens are apostrophized in line 5, and night and day personified in subsequent lines (a conventional contrary in Senecan — and Elizabethan — soliloquy). Lines 5, 6 and 7 offer the repetition of appositives ("deed . . . attempt . . . murder"), a custom much seen in Shakespeare, too. (Cf. Hamlet's "the whips and scorns of time, / The oppressor's wrong, the proud man's contumely," – III.i.70-71, in his fourth soliloquy.) Charged adjectives appear in nearly every line. In sum, Hieronimo's oration is primarily rhetorical device. Many, if not all, of these materials may be seen in a soliloquy written by Seneca himself, in which Atreus opens the second episode of *Thyestes* with the following:

> Spiritless, nerveless, spineless, and (what I consider a tyrant's worst reproach in high issues) vengeanceless, are you passing your time in idle plaints after so many injuries? . . . The whole world should be clashing arms by now, navies should be scouring both the twin seas, city and countryside should be blazing flames and drawn swords sparkle on every side.[29]

Here is also visible (even though in prose, not verse) a speech full of highly charged adjectives, of repetitive language ("Spiritless, nerveless, spineless"), of exaggerated conceits ("The whole world should be clashing arms"). Figures of speech abound ("navies . . . scouring both the twin seas"), and contraries rise up at every hand, as in later words of the speech where Atreus says of his brother, "He will either destroy or perish," or speaks of "a deed no posterity can approve but none ignore."

The soliloquy of Seneca's Atreus ends in a homiletic self-bolstering:

> He will either destroy or perish; the crime is the prize for the man who seizes the initiative.[30]

Atreus is dealing with a Hobson's choice, with the less despicable of alternatives.

In Marlowe's *Faustus*, the devils show a general awareness of the conventions of morality drama. Yet Faustus himself resembles a character-portrayal from early Shakespeare much more than a stage-stereotype from the moralities. At the stroke of eleven he is seen winding down the play:

> Ah, Faustus,
> Now hast thou but one bare hour to live,
> And then thou must be damned perpetually!
> Stand still, you ever-moving spheres of heaven,
> That time may cease and midnight never come.
> Fair Nature's eye, rise, rise again, and make
> Perpetual day; or let this hour be but
> A year, a month, a week, a natural day,
> That Faustus may repent and save his soul!
>
> (V.ii)[31]

This speech, serving both to inform the audience that the rebel's time has come and to furnish an introspection of the character in his remorse, bears the stamp of Senecan rhetorical flight in its apostrophe to the heavens, yet one is reminded of T. S. Eliot's statement here: "Certainly, Elizabethan bombast can be traced to Seneca; Elizabethans themselves ridiculed the Senecan imitation. But if we reflect, not on the more grotesque exaggerations, but on the dramatic poetry of the first half of the period, as a whole, we see that Seneca had as much to do with its merits and its progress as with its faults and its delays. Certainly it is all 'rhetorical,' but if it had not been rhetorical, would it have been anything? . . . Without bombast, we should not have had *King Lear*. The art of dramatic speech, we must remember, is as near to oratory as to ordinary speech or to other poetry.[32] Senecan though it may be in the main, Faustus' speech is one of the most eloquent of pre-Shakespearean soliloquies. It is highly alliterative, but certainly free from awkward alliterations, and apostrophe aside it is free from most other obviousness of poetic technique. Its rhythm (Marlowe's "mighty line") is not immediately apparent as entirely regularized blank verse. Phrases such as "you ever-moving spheres of heaven" excluded, it has the inevitability of "realistic speech," a quality of diction certainly not attributable to the earlier quoted speech of Hieronimo (or to some soliloquies in early Shakespeare analyzed in later chapters here). In brief, the speech of Faustus, like those cited from Kyd's play, exemplifies soliloquy of a drama transitional between the late moralities and the earliest Shakespeare, a body of plays fusing medieval and Elizabethan craft and therefore melding soliloquy content and form of both eras.

Notes

Chapter III

[1] Quotations from *Nature* are taken from John S. Farmer, ed., *Early English Dramatists: Recently Recovered "Lost" Tudor Plays* (1907; rpt. New York: 1966), p. 84.

[2] John M. Manly, ed., *Specimens of the Pre-Shaksperean Drama* (Boston: 1925), I, 315-16.

[3] Robert B. Heilman, *An Anthology of English Drama Before Shakespeare* (New York: 1952), p. 76.

[4] Robert Dodsley, *A Select Collection of Old English Plays*, 4th ed. by W. Carew Hazlitt (1874-76; rpt. New York: 1964), II, 89-90.

[5] Bevington (p. 796) dates the play as c. 1405-25. Chambers (II, 437) says Pollard dates it "not later than the middle of the reign of Henry VI." (Henry ruled England twice, from 1422 to 1461 and again, briefly, 1470-71.) Edgar T. Schell and J. D. Shuchter, eds., *English Morality Plays and Moral Interludes* (New York: 1969), p. 1, say c. 1350-99.

[6] *English Morality Plays and Moral Interludes*, eds. Edgar T. Schell and J. D. Shuchter (New York: 1969), p. 11.

[7] Philip Henderson, ed., *The Complete Poems of John Skelton*, 2nd, rev. ed. (London and Toronto: 1948), pp. 178-80. All quotations from Skelton's *Magnificence* are taken from Henderson.

[8] Henderson, *Skelton*, p. 187.

[9] Henderson, *Skelton*, p. 228.

[10] Henderson, *Skelton*, p. 235.

[11] Farmer, *Dramatists*, p. 329. All quotations from *Impatient Poverty* are taken from Farmer, pp. 329-42.

[12] Dodsley, *Old English Plays*, II, 45. All quotations from *Lusty Juventus* are from Dodsley.

[13] All Bible quotations are from The King James Version.

[14] *The Dartmouth Bible*, eds. Roy B. Chamberlin and Herman Feldman,

2nd ed., rev. and enlarged (Boston: 1961), p. 819.

[15] Dodsley, *Old English Plays*, II, 62-63.

[16] Dodsley, *Old English Plays*, II, 68-69.

[17] Dodsley, *Old English Plays*, II, 89-91.

[18] *Engl. Morality Plays and Moral Interludes*, pp. 414-15.

[19] Willard Farnham, in *The Medieval Heritage of Elizabethan Tragedy* (Oxford: 1963), passim, develops the thesis that the English stage, under Elizabeth, was peculiar in Europe in its close adherence to its medieval heritage.

[20] So labeled by Bernard Spivack in *Shakespeare and the Allegory of Evil*, passim.

[21] Farnham, *Heritage*, p. 209.

[22] Farnham, *Heritage*, p. 251.

[23] Dodsley, *Old English Plays*, IV, 128.

[24] Spivack, p. 272.

[25] Preface to *Christopher Marlowe's Doctor Faustus: Text and Major Criticism* (New York: 1966), p. vii.

[26] Heilman, *Anthol. of Engl. Drama*, pp. 281-82.

[27] Heilman, *Anthol. of Engl. Drama*, p. 286.

[28] Clemen, *Tragedy*, p. 238.

[29] Seneca, *Thyestes*, trans. Moses Hadas (Indianapolis: 1957), p. 7.

[30] Seneca, *Thyestes*, p. 7.

[31] *Christopher Marlowe's Doctor Faustus*, p. 55.

[32] Introduction to *Seneca, His Tenne Tragedies*, p. xxxvii.

Chapter IV

Shakespearean: Its Content

The very bulk of Shakespearean soliloquy requiring division and considerable volume for effective review, this chapter will concentrate only on its content. Here content is differentiated from structures (including language per se). It is also considered separately from any evolution of qualities visible within the canon.

The content, inescapably informative, is three-fold: exposition of plot (over-all plot-action, or merely role-action), homily, and character revelation. The first occurs in all soliloquy; homily appears initially in medieval drama. But Shakespeare developed, virtually alone, a distinct type only hinted at in the Middle Ages, the psychological soliloquy. And he put it to use constantly for revealing motivation or intention of his characters or for laying bare the war within a personality (as distinguished from an abstraction-persona).

While it is true that the ultimate basis of this innovation lies in medieval soliloquies of speaker-identification and in the psychomachic *debat* of the morality plays, Shakespeare so highly refined his soliloquies of character as to render practically unrecognizable their relationship to any earlier variety of solo utterance. Notwithstanding the remarkable originality of his psychological soliloquies, Shakespeare's utilization of medieval materials and forms is approximately equal, in quantity at least, to his original additions to soliloquy. The medieval inheritance is especially evident in the homiletic content of Shakespearean soliloquy, although also visible in his soliloquies of plot exposition. On the other hand, as Muriel Bradbrook says, in *Elizabethan Stage Conditions* (Cambr., England: 1932), p. 6: "The Elizabethan stage had no rules: even those tacitly observed, like Lawrence's law of re-entry, may never have been conscious, much less formulated. The fact that investigators have to reconstruct what the dramatists merely accepted tends to make them more conscious of their formulae." Bradbrook is doubtless correct, and this study does not mean to suggest for one moment that Shakespeare was writing soliloquies in accordance with some body of regulation formulated for the Elizabethan stage. It does suggest, strongly, that his uses of soliloquy were often within a main stream of dramatic tradition at least as old as morality drama, i.e., the conscious employment of soliloquy for definite purposes of plot exposition and homily.

To speak of three-fold use of soliloquy is not to describe three completely disparate soliloquy types. Most Shakespearean soliloquies, like their forebears, simultaneously perform more than one function. Exposition of over-all plot, or of role action, and homily are very often combined, inseparably, in the same speech, and character-soliloquy usually includes at least one of the other two elements as well. This overlapping is clear in a soliloquy which contains all three elements, the Bastard's speech on Commodity (II.i.561-98) from *King John*:

> Mad world! Mad Kings! Mad composition!
> John, to stop Arthur's title in the whole,
> Hath willingly departed with a part.
> And France, whose armor Conscience buckled on,
> Whom Zeal and Charity brought to the field
> As God's own soldier, rounded in the ear
> With that same purpose changer, that sly Devil,
> That broker that still breaks the pate of faith,
> That daily break-vow — he that wins of all,
> Of kings, of beggars, old men, young men, maids,
> Who, having no external thing to lose
> But the word "maid," cheats the poor maid of that —
> That smooth-faced gentleman, tickling Commodity,
> Commodity, the bias of the world —
> The world, who of itself is peisèd well,
> Made to run even upon even ground,
> Till this advantage, this vile-drawing bias,
> This sway of motion, this Commodity,
> Makes it take head from all indifferency,
> From all direction, purpose, course, intent —
> And this same bias, this Commodity,
> This bawd, this broker, this all-changing word,
> Clapped on the outward eye of fickle France,
> Hath drawn him from his own determined aid,
> From a resolved and honorable war
> To a most base and vile-concluded peace.
> And why rail I on this Commodity?
> But for because he hath not wooed me yet,
> Not that I have the power to clutch my hand
> When his fair angels would salute my palm,
> But for my hand, as unattempted yet,
> Like a poor beggar raileth on the rich.
> Well, whiles I am a beggar, I will rail
> And say there is no sin but to be rich;
> And being rich, my virtue then shall be

> To say there is no vice but beggary.
> Since kings break faith upon commodity,
> Gain, be my lord, for I will worship thee.

The initial lines of this soliloquy offer exposition of plot-action; Faulconbridge informs the audience of some of the results of the negotiations between his king, John, and the French forces ("John . . ./ Hath willingly departed with a part"). These same lines also comprise an introduction of sorts into the main homiletic content of the piece: the Bastard is making moral judgments within this plot explanation, and obviously disapproves of the concessions made by John and of the motives of both John and Philip of France ("rounded in the ear/ With that same purpose changer . . . Commodity") as exhibited in their parley. Lines 573-80 constitute the major part of one of Shakespeare's best known homilies; their content is self-explanatory (as is that of most homiletic soliloquies):

> Commodity, the bias of the world —

Cleverness of wording, not ideological subtlety, is the hallmark of homiletic soliloquy. At line 581 the speech begins to revert back to a more personal tone, to a combination of exposition of plot and character revelation, and Philip begins to explain both the plot and his own character in the query:

> And why rail I on this Commodity? (1. 587)

His eleven-line reply (11. 588-98) combines prediction of his future course of action and exposure of the motivation for it:

> Since kings break faith upon commodity,
> Gain, be my lord, for I will worship thee.
>
> (11. 597-98)

Taken as a whole the soliloquy reveals his character to be that of a man of considerable shrewdness of observation who can adapt his behavior on demand. Portions of this soliloquy, then, illustrate each of the three leading sorts of disclosure in Shakespearean soliloquy, usually in combination, once or twice separately. For convenience alone, these three varieties are examined separately in this chapter, as plot exposition, homily, and character revelation.

Plot Exposition

Christian drama has been, from the first, a drama of intrigue. Intrigue required a reliable means of exposition, and soliloquy provided such a medium from the first, as witnessed within the numerous examples of medieval soliloquy presented in Chapters ii and iii. That Shakespeare continued the employment of the medieval instrument is plainly obvious, other considerations aside, simply in the great frequency of the word "show" and its synonyms in his soliloquies.

Professor Clemen emphasizes Shakespeare's acknowledgment of the demands of intrigue on expository soliloquy, in citing the medieval tradition of expository set speeches where a character introduces himself in some detail and at the same time prepares the assemblage for future action. In this regard Clemen writes: "This convention remains the basis of Gloucester's opening soliloquy in Shakespeare's *Richard III*, where Gloucester's introduction of himself is combined with a partial revelation of his own designs and some account of the present state of affairs."[1]

Soliloquies of plot exposition are sub-divided into two kinds (detailed so much earlier in this study as conceivably to need review at this juncture), sometimes combined in the same speech: declamations of plot-action which inform the audience about the over-all action of the play, and role-action speeches, in which personae announce to the audience their own present or imminent action in the plot. The latter are to be distinguished from soliloquies of homiletic self-exposure (personae identifying themselves as representatives of evil), and from character-revelation soliloquies (psychological soliloquies) in which personae explain the psychological nature of their roles, as to motivation, intent, or psychomachic internal debate. These other types will be detailed in the closing section of this chapter.

Very often the Shakespearean soliloquy of plot-action will afford a brief opening or closing to an act or scene. Imogen opens the sixth scene in *Cymbeline* in such a way:

> A father cruel, and a stepdame false,
> A foolish suitor to a wedded lady,
> That hath her husband banished. Oh, that husband!
> My supreme crown of grief! And those repeated
> Vexations of it! Had I been thief-stol'n,
> As my two brothers, happy! But most miserable
> Is the desire that's glorious. Blest be those,
> How mean soe'er, that have their honest wills,
> Which seasons comfort. (I.vi.1-9)

The playwright has combined his little summary of the play's beginning with a homily ("Blest be those . . .") in the gnomic final three lines. *Cymbeline* abounds in short soliloquies of plot-action — further instance is provided by the soliloquy of the Second Lord, at the end of the opening scene of Act II:

> That such a crafty devil as is his mother
> Should yield the world this ass! A woman that
> Bears all down with her brain, and this her son
> Cannot take two from twenty, for his heart,
> And leave eighteen. Alas, poor Princess,

> Thou divine Imogen, what thou endurest
> Betwixt a father by thy stepdame governed,
> A mother hourly coining plots, a wooer
> More hateful than the foul expulsion is
> Of thy dear husband, than that horrid act
> Of the divorce he'd make! The Heavens hold firm
> The walls of thy dear honor, keep unshaked
> That temple, thy fair mind, that thou mayst stand
> To enjoy thy banished lord and this great land!
> (II.i.57-70)

Here, the Second Lord seems to be serving practically as a one-man cheering section for the wronged Imogen, that she may not falter in her goodness and patience. Notable, too, is the similarity in content between this speech and that quoted just previously, both being little more than recapitulations of the plot to the points of the play where the respective soliloquies occur. Additional examples of mere plot-summary in soliloquy appear in Imogen's opening of Act III, Scene vi (1-27), in that of Cloten beginning Act IV (i.1-30), and in another by Imogen in Act IV, Scene ii (291-332), a long revelation to the audience of her positive identification of the headless body of her husband Posthumus — a false "revelation," by the way, eventually adding surprise to the play. Posthumus himself delivers a similar updating of plot on waking from his dream in Scene iv of Act V (123-51). He is given a letter to read aloud to an empty stage.

Often a role-action soliloquy is delivered by the chief personage. The plays of Shakespeare are full of such soliloquies setting forth eloquent and explicit explanations of the actions or the physical circumstances of the leading figure. Romeo's soliloquy of death is such a speech. Its information consists of three principal parts, Romeo's interment of Paris in the monument, his "Thou art not conquered" speech (in utter dramatic irony), and his closing notification to the audience of his death. The last of the three parts follows:

> Arms, take your last embrace! And lips, O you
> The doors of breath, seal with a righteous kiss
> A dateless bargain to engrossing death!
> Come, bitter conduct, come, unsavory guide!
> Thou desperate pilot, now at once run on
> The dashing rocks thy seasick weary bark.
> Here's to my love! [Drinks] O true apothecary!
> Thy drugs are quick. Thus with a kiss I die. [Dies]
> (V.iii.113-20)

The symbolic toast, the allusion to the apothecary who has sold Romeo the poison, and the closing word "die" render this speech fully explanatory of Romeo's suicide, and present the information through a combining of overt act with demonstrative word.

The speech by Macbeth in Act III, Scene i, concluding the examples of plot-exposition soliloquy, certainly recapitulates much of the over-all plot action ("They hailed him father to a line of kings."), and some of Macbeth's own actions ("I murdered"), within all of Macbeth's apprehensive conjectures about Banquo:

> To be thus is nothing,
> But to be safely thus.
> Our fears in Banquo
> Stick deep, and in his royalty of nature
> Reigns that which would be feared.
> . . . .
> There is none but he
> Whose being I do fear. And under him
> My Genius is rebuked, as it is said
> Mark Antony's was by Caesar. He chid the sisters
> When first they put the name of King upon me,
> And bade them speak to him. Then prophetlike
> They hailed him father to a line of kings.
> Upon my head they placed a fruitless crown
> And put a barren scepter in my gripe,
> Thence to be wrenched with an unlineal hand,
> No son of mine succeeding. If 't be so,
> For Banquo's issue have I filed my mind
> For them the gracious Duncan have I murdered,
> Put rancors in the vessel of my peace
> Only for them, and mine eternal jewel
> Given to the common enemy of man
> To make them kings — the seed of Banquo kings!
> Rather than so, come, Fate, into the list,
> And champion me to the utterance! (III.i.48-72)

Plot-exposition soliloquies abound in Shakespeare, among them Gloucester's "winter of our discontent" opening of *Richard III* (I.i.1-41), briefly cited above, via Clemen, and Juliet's "What's in a name" soliloquy (II.ii.38-48), which Romeo overhears undiscovered by the musing Juliet.

Homily

Taken to task by Voltaire for failing the Unities (later excused by Pope and Johnson), Shakespeare had not, however, failed the dictum of Horace that poetry must both please and profit. Nor is didacticism in Shakespeare, when present, seldom far below the surface. One of the pillars of Shakespearean didactic soliloquy is homily. His three principal uses of it may be named for convenience Mini-homily (usually shorter than twenty lines, beginning or ending a scene or act, its primary function often structural); Grand Homily (a leading figure developing a major homiletic theme, in a speech usually longer than twenty lines); and, lastly, soliloquies of Homiletic Self-exposure (best exemplified through Aaron the Moor, Richard III, and Iago). All three of these come directly from Shakespeare's medieval forebears, which are illustrated at length within the preceding chapters. Mini-homily, however, is much more frequent in Shakespeare, relatively speaking, than in medieval plays, where homily does not customarily function also as a structural element for opening or closing divisions of a play.

A discussion of Mini-homily need not become mired in the question as to which plays are separated into acts and scenes in the First Folio or in other early editions. As is well known, the plays of Shakespeare, and of other Elizabethan dramatists, were normally presented without a break from beginning to end. The word "scene" is used here to indicate both the artificial units of time and action in the source edition (G. B. Harrison's *Complete Works*) and unitings of speech, action, and locale which in themselves logically dictate the amount of stage-time and number of lines constituting a separable "scene." Mini-homily, to define it more thoroughly, affords a homily (of usually fewer than twenty lines, as stated) at the beginning or ending of a scene, sometimes seeming principally structural in purpose, as when providing fillip to a scene in a rhymed scene-tag, and sometimes appearing to be mainly a concession to the tradition of didacticism in drama. Mini-homily may or may not be rhymed; no formula applies here. These brief homilies which begin or end a scene are not usually among the most notable of Shakespeare's soliloquies. Their main importance (other than didactic, that is) often appears to be as structural link in the play. The samplings in this chapter have been segregated as scene-openers and scene enders.

Several such entries perform two or three functions simultaneously, as is frequently the case in all types of Shakespearean soliloquy. An instance of this is the four-line speech uttered by Lady Macbeth early in Act III. The soliloquy does not actually open its separate scene (ii), to be exact, but for all practical considerations it opens a structural unit of the play, being preceded by only three lines which serve to dismiss a servant. The speech follows:

> Naught's had, all's spent,
> Where our desire is got without content.
> 'Tis safer to be that which we destroy
> Than by destruction dwell in doubtful joy.
>
> (III.ii.4–7)

The monitory tone is immediately apparent ("'Tis safer to be . . ."). The dramatic import lies, no doubt, in the indication that Lady Macbeth now has recognized the "doubtful joy" of being implicated in murder, the soliloquy thus serving the dual use of generalized homily and of enlightening the playgoers as to the doubts of Lady Macbeth (the latter also aiding in characterization).

A second instance of Mini-homily (of the many from which one might choose) is in the seventeen lines spoken by Angelo as an opening for Scene iv of the second act of *Measure*. Although its bulk is concerned principally with plot-line and revelation of character and also serves to introduce both the scene-unit and the tone of that scene, its final four lines, quoted here, are devoted to homily:

> O place, O form,
> How often dost thou with thy case, thy habit,
> Wrench awe from fools, and tie the wiser souls
> To thy false seeming! (II.iv.12-15)

Here is a little homily on being seduced by the attractions of high position.

A third Mini-homily is in the nine-line speech by Edgar opening Act IV of *Lear*:

> Yet better thus, and known to be contemned,
> Than still contemned and flattered. To be worst,
> The lowest and most dejected thing of fortune,
> Stands still in esperance, lives not in fear.
> The lamentable change is from the best,
> The worst returns to laughter. Welcome then,
> Thou unsubstantial air that I embrace!
> The wretch that thou has blown unto the worst
> Owes nothing to thy blasts. (IV.i.1-9)

Egdar's sentiment here that the man already at the bottom of fortune's ladder aspires only to the better since he need no longer fear the worst is at least somewhat reminiscent of statements soliloquized by another scorned personage, Parolles, in *All's Well*, cited further on as example of Grand Homily:

> Simply the thing I am
> Shall make me live.
> . . . .
> And, Parolles, live
> Safest in shame! Being fooled, by foolery thrive!
> (IV.iii.369-75)

Edgar closes Scene vi of Act III in *Lear* with a fourteen-line Mini-homily:

> When we our betters see bearing our woes,
> We scarcely think our miseries our foes.
> Who alone suffers suffers most i' the mind,
> Leaving free things and happy shows behind.

> But then the mind much sufferance doth o'erskip
> When grief hath mates, and bearing fellowship.
> How light and portable my pain seems now
> When that which makes me bend makes the King bow,
> He childed as I fathered! Tom, away!
> Mark the high noises, and thyself bewray
> When false opinion, whose wrong thought defiles thee,
> In thy just proof repeals and reconciles thee.
> What will hap more tonight, safe 'scape the King!
> Lurk, lurk. (11. 109-22)

Taken as a whole this soliloquy has a two-fold purpose; its final half-dozen lines serve as information about the imminent action of Edgar ("Lurk, lurk"), while the opening portion ("Who alone suffers") operates as homily, advising that misery loves company.

Neither Mini-homily nor Grand Homily is restricted to any one phase of Shakespeare's playwriting. In the early *Richard III*, the scrivener delivers a fourteen-line opening for Act III, Scene vi, which performs the double task of first giving plot description ("This is the indictment") and then passing moral judgment ("such bad dealing") on the action thus described:

> This is the indictment of the good Lord Hastings,
> Which in a set hand fairly is engrossed,
> That is may be this day read o'er in Paul's
> And mark how well the sequel hangs together.
> Eleven hours I spent to write it over,
> For yesternight by Catesby was it brought me.
> The precedent was full as long a-doing.
> And yet within these five hours lived Lord Hastings,
> Untainted, unexamined, free, at liberty.
> Here's a good world the while! Why, who's so gross,
> That seeth not this palpable device?
> Yet who's so blind but says he sees it not?
> Bad is the world, and all will come to naught
> When such bad dealing must be seen in thought.
>   (11. 1-14)

And in *I Henry VI*, from the very beginning of the career, Act IV, Scene i is closed by a thirteen-line Mini-homily of Thomas Beaufort, Duke of Exeter:

> Well didst thou, Richard, to suppress thy voice,
> For, had the passions of thy heart burst out,
> I fear we should have seen deciphered there
> More rancorous spite, more furious raging broils,
> Than yet can be imagined or supposed.

> But howsoe'er, no simple man that sees
> This jarring discord of nobility,
> This shouldering of each other in the Court,
> This factious bandying of their favorites,
> But that it doth presage some ill event.
> 'Tis much when scepters are in children's hands,
> But more when envy breeds unkind division;
> There comes the ruin, there begins confusion.
>
> (11. 182-94)

The soliloquy is only figuratively addressed to Richard, Duke of York: he has just left the scene. It is of course really addressed to the play's viewers, and the "Well done!" bestowed on York by Exeter is all part of its homiletic tone, which certainly supplies effective closure to a long scene.

Even Falstaff's famed soliloquy on honor in the fairly early (1597) *I Henry IV* may conceivably be included within the category of Mini-homily, since it may be viewed as a sixteen-line homiletic fillip for its scene (V.i.128-43). However, the dramatic and philosophic impact of its seeming negation of honor may well qualify the declaration for many readers as Grand Homily (leading figure, major theme).

As affirmed above, no over-all conclusion is possible concerning rhyme in Mini-homily. The speech by Lady Macbeth quoted above is in quite regular blank verse, whereas the fourteen lines quoted from Edgar (III.vi.109-22) are rhymed in somewhat irregular iambic. On the other hand, the nine-line homily cited from Edgar (IV.i.1-9) is not rhymed, nor is the scene-opener of Angelo (II.iv.12-15). General conclusions regarding Mini-homily can be made, however, as to brevity, content, positioning in scenes, and frequency of structural operation. And Mini-homily is much more numerous in the plays than Grand Homily; these specimens are only a few from among the myriad.

Grand Homily is not really frequent in Shakespeare, but when it occurs it is readily recognizable from its content and the prominence of its speaker. It may be defined as a relatively long soliloquy (usually more than twenty lines) of major homiletic theme delivered by a key figure in the action. In sum, the significance of Grand Homily is mainly thematic rather than scene-setting, as evidenced by its occurrence so often in memorable speeches. Even when on occasion it may come at the beginning or end of a scene, it does not appear to be utilized mainly as structural integrant or fillip, as Mini-homily so many times does.

Grand Homily may be found throughout the plays. To offer examples in chronological order, the soliloquy on Commodity by Faulconbridge in *King John* (dated by Harrison as c. 1596), is a prime Grand Homily from the early period. Its homiletic concerns were explored at the onset of this chapter, pp. 155-58, illustrating overlapped ingredients in Shakespearean soliloquy. Suffice to say here that it is delivered by a prominent figure in the play, is relatively quite long (thirty-eight lines), and espouses a signficant homiletic theme ("Commodity, the bias of the world").

A second Grand Homily, from the middle of the career, is the eleven-line utterance by Parolles at the close of Scene iii in the fourth act of *All's Well* (dated by Harrison as "'somewhere between 1601 and 1604'"). Earlier cited briefly in this chapter, the speech reads in full:

> Yet am I thankful. If my heart were great,
> 'Twould burst at this. Captain I'll be no more,
> But I will eat, and drink, and sleep as soft
> As captain shall. Simply the thing I am
> Shall make me live. Who knows himself a braggart,
> Let him fear this, for it will come to pass
> That every braggart shall be found an ass.
> Rust, sword! Cool, blushes! And, Parolles, live
> Safest in shame! Being fooled, by foolery thrive!
> There's place and means for every man alive.
>   (11. 366-75)

If compactness and scene-closing position indicate relationship to Mini-homily, the sweepingly philosophical tenor of "Simply the thing I am/ Shall make me live" and of "There's place and means for every man alive" certainly advertise this speech of Parolles as Grand Homily: taken at face value, here is an assurance that for every man alive, even for shameful braggarts, there is proper place and means for survival in this world.

Posthumus has a Grand Homily occupying the entire fifth scene in Act II of *Cymbeline*, from Shakespeare's late period (prob. 1610):

> Is there no way for men to be, but women
> Must be half-workers? We are all bastards,
> And that most venerable man which I
> Did call my father was I know not where
> When I was stamped. Some coiner with his tools
> Made me a counterfeit. Yet my mother seemed
> The Dian of that time: so doth my wife
> The nonpareil of this. Oh, vengeance, vengeance!
> Me of my lawful pleasure she restrained,
> And prayed me oft forbearance; did it with
> A pudency so rosy, the sweet view on 't
> Might well have warmed old Saturn, that I thought her
> As chaste as unsunned snow. Oh, all the devils!
> This yellow Iachimo in an hour — was 't not? —
> Or less — at first? — perchance he spoke not, but

> Like a full-acorned boar, a German one,
> Cried "Oh!" and mounted, found no opposition
> But what he looked for should oppose and she
> Should from encounter guard. Could I find out
> The woman's part in me! For there's no motion
> That tends to vice in man but I affirm
> It is the woman's part. Be it lying, note it
> The woman's; flattering, hers; deceiving, hers;
> Lust and rank thoughts, hers, hers; revenges, hers;
> Ambitions, covetings, change of prides, disdain,
> Nice longing, slanders, mutability,
> All faults that may be named, nay, that Hell knows,
> Why, hers, in part or all, but rather all.
> For even to vice
> They are not constant, but are changing still
> One vice, but of a minute old, for one
> Not half so old as that. I'll write against them,
> Detest them, curse them. Yet 'tis greater skill
> In a true hate to pray they have their will.
> The very devils cannot plague them better.
>
> (11. 1-35)

The concluding sixteen lines above are a warning against women's wiles ("flattering . . . deceiving . . . mutability"). The anti-feminism in the speech is no more felicitous than the misanthropy in another Grand Homily from the same late period, Timon's soliloquy (IV.iii.1-47) cursing mankind in general. That homily is merely excerpted here, to exhibit how its bitter tone echoes that of Posthumus. *Vide* Timon:

> The learnèd pate
> Ducks to the golden fool. . . . (11. 17-18)

A final illustration of Grand Homily is taken from the very end of the canon, Wolsey's "Farewell to all my greatness!" in *Henry VIII*:

> So farewell to the little good you bear me.
> Farewell! A long farewell, to all my greatness!
> This is the state of man: Today he puts forth
> The tender leaves of hopes; tomorrow blossoms
> And bears his blushing honors thick upon him;
> The third day comes a frost, a killing frost,
> And, when he thinks, good easy man, full surely
> His greatness is aripening, nips his root,
> And then he falls as I do. I have ventured,
> Like little wanton boys that swim on bladders,
> This many summers in a sea of glory,
> But far beyond my depth. My high-blown pride

> At length broke under me, and now has left me,
> Weary and old with service, to the mercy
> Of a rude stream that must forever hide me.
> Vain pomp and glory of this world, I hate ye.
> I feel my heart new opened. Oh, how wretchèd
> Is that poor man that hangs on princes' favors!
> There is, betwixt that smile we would aspire to,
> That sweet aspéct of princes, and their ruin,
> More pangs and fears than wars or women have.
> And when he falls, he falls like Lucifer,
> Never to hope again. (III.ii.350-72)

Wolsey's initial metaphor of new leaves, blossoms and frost of course opens a thorough admonition on the fragility of high place, a concept not far removed from that in the Mini-homily of Angelo cited from *Measure* (II.iv.12-15).

As to homiletic self-exposure, three of Shakespeare's characters come immediately to mind for soliloquizing on themselves as potential or real evil in the flesh — Aaron the Moor, the Duke of Gloucester (later to be Richard III), and Iago. All three of these villains display Shakespeare in doubtless his most medieval mantle, through the repetition in their utterances, sometimes virtually verbatim, of speeches derived from morality Vice personae.

Aaron is not much heard in soliloquy: his best known lines are addressed to others. But there is one soliloquy, beginning Act II, Scene iii, where Aaron reveals himself a representative of "villainy" [his word]; the speech is patently drawn to relate the true nature of Aaron. Indeed, it resembles nothing so much as the labeling of abstract characters in the morality tradition; in a sense, Aaron has a banner hanging out of his mouth announcing his function in the play.

> He that had wit would think that I had none,
> To bury so much gold under a tree
> And never after to inherit it.
> Let him that thinks of me so abjectly
> Know that this gold must coin a stratagem,
> Which, cunningly effected, will beget
> A very excellent piece of villainy.
> And so repose, sweet gold, for their unrest.
>
> (II.iii.1-8)

This boast of Aaron may be compared to the vaunt of Belial in *The Castle of Perseverance*, an early morality cited for other reasons in Chapter iii:

> What folk that I grope, they gapen and grin.
> Iwis, from Carlisle into Kent my carping they take.

> Both the back and the buttock bursteth all on brenne
> With works of wreche. I work them mickle wrake;
> In woe is all my wenne. (11. 200-04)²

With "wrake" and "wenne" respectively glossed as "harm" and "delight," Belial, too, in the final two lines here, is exulting in "a very excellent piece of villainy," indeed, in many such "pieces." Resemblance between Belial and Aaron is clear, in that each announces himself as perpetrator of "villainy."

None of the three villains of Shakespeare makes more visible his insidious intentions and prideful depravity than Richard III. Richard is directly descended from the medieval Vice abstraction seen also in Aaron the Moor and Iago.³ Richard opens the drama of which he is the title character with the notorious soliloquy of "the winter of our discontent" (I.i.1-40), early announcing that he is

> determined to prove a villain. (I.i.30)

In John Bale's Interlude *Kynge Johan* (c. 1538), not, strictly speaking, a morality play but contemporary of and replete in the formulas of the moralities, the character Dissimulacyon says almost the same thing to his friend Sedycyon:

> To hold all thynges vp I play my part now and than.
> . . . .
> Thowgh we playe the knavys, we must shew a good pretence;
> (11. 681 and 687)⁴

The sense of the second line here ("play the knave") is obviously that of Richard's "prove a villain."

Shortly after having announced it, Richard reinforces his determination by telling, in another soliloquy, of specific villainy he is about to perform:

> Simple, plain Clarence! I do love thee so
> That I will shortly send thy soul to Heaven,
> If Heaven will take the present at our hands.
> (I.i.118-20)

Quite aside from the overt plot instruction in the speech, cynicism is inherent in its concluding line. Heaven's acceptance of "the present" makes no difference to Richard: he will fearlessly dispatch his brother George, Duke of Clarence, whatever the Deity's proscriptions against fratricide. Here again Richard's medieval Vice lineage gleams forth.

A bit later on, Anne accosts Richard with the following:

> Villain, thou know'st no law of God nor man.

> No beast so fierce but knows some touch of pity. (I.ii.70-71)

But her remarks are rendered practically redundant, when the Duke himself utters the following words in soliloquy in the next scene:

> Having God, her conscience, and these bars against me,
> And I nothing to back my suit at all
> But the plain Devil and dissembling looks,
>
> (I.ii.235-37)

Dissimulacyon, in Bale's *Kynge Johan*, approximately fifty-five years previous, sounds very much like this when he proclaims:

> Thowgh I seme a shepe, I can play the suttle fox; (1. 713)

Richard has once again identified with the Vice tradition. Like Aaron and Iago, Richard is that morality abstraction, slightly modernized for the Elizabethan stage, as he explains yet again in soliloquy in the subsequent scene:

> I do the wrong, and first begin to brawl.
> The secret mischiefs that I set abroach
> I lay unto the grievous charge of others.
> Clarence, whom I indeed have laid in darkness,
> I do beweep to many simple gulls —
> Namely, to Hastings, Derby, Buckingham —
> And say it is the Queen and her allies
> That stir the King against the Duke my brother.
> Now, they believe it, and withal whet me
> To be revenged on Rivers, Vaughan, Grey.
> But then I sigh, and with a piece of Scripture
> Tell them that God bids us do good for evil.
> And thus I clothe my naked villainy
> With old odd ends stolen out of Holy Writ,
> And seem a saint when most I play the devil.
>
> (I.iii.324-38)

How openly Richard again reveals here that he is indeed the Vice, invoking any useful means, Christian or other (false testimony, reverent sighing, "a piece of Scripture," "odd ends stolen out of Holy Writ") to his anti-Christian end, that is, to "play the devil."

Iago appears no less and no more an overt descendant of the Vice than Richard. As for his dissembling, one of the key postulates for linking Shakespeare's villains to the morality tradition, Iago gives an obvious forecast in:

> I am not what I am. (I.i.65)

G. R. Elliott, in his book on *Othello* entitled *Flaming Minister* (Durham:

1953), p. 76, says that Iago, in the first scene of Act II, "plumes up his evil will . . . by conceiving himself as a channel of impersonal evil, assigning now to himself the 'knavery' he tried to read into Cassio . . . ." Surely, Iago *is* a channel of impersonal evil, portrayed, like the Vice figures with whom he and the other two villains of this chapter are compared, as fully aware of his evil identity. Witness again the open "vaunts" uttered by each one of the Shakespearean villains (Aaron. Richard and Iago), Professor Elliott makes it a question of Iago's conscience, illustrated, he says on p. 206, in Iago's "He [Cassio] hath a daily beauty in his life/ That makes me ugly" soliloquy. "Iago's final soliloquy [V.i.11-22] . . . shows his suppressed conscience making a final and extraordinary protest." For the purposes of this study, the character's conscience is irrelevant; in fact, these three villains are displayed as having no conscience, as pre-psychological stage types rather than "human" dramatis personae. What "conscience" can there be in a dramatic character who is made to say:

> And what's he then that says I play the villain?
> When this advice is free I give and honest,
> Probal to thinking, and indeed the course
> To win the Moor again?
> . . . .
> Divinity of Hell!
> When devils will the blackest sins put on,
> They do suggest at first with heavenly shows,
> As I do now. (II.iii.342-45, 356-59)

Is this not rather the morality persona Dissimulacyon proclaiming in Bale's *Kynge Johan*:

> Thowgh we playe the knavys, we must shew a good pretence.
> (1. 687)

and in a direct line from the boast expressed by Belial in *The Castle of Perseverance*:

> I work them mickle wrake;
> In woe is all my wenne. (11. 203-04)

As for parallels, the opening line of this Iago soliloquy ("And what's he then that says I play the villain?") hearkens back almost verbatim, although interrogative in form, to the soliloquy in which Gloucester opens *Richard III*:

> I am determined to prove a villain. (I.i.30)

And Iago later reveals the duplicity inherent in this question ("And what's he then that says I play the villain?"), when he affirms his villainy openly in soliloquy in Act IV:

> Work on,

My medicine, work! Thus credulous fools are caught.
(IV.i.45-46)

A major stylistic parallelism in the three plays heaves into sight here, in addition to structural and thematic parallelism among the three villains, Aaron, Richard and Iago. The parallel in style lies in the frequency with which the three Shakespearean descendants of the Vice echo the statements of one another. Each villain utters at least one vaunt, in the best morality-play tradition, and each identifies himself in words very similar to those of the others. Richard is "determined to prove a villain"; Aaron boasts of "a very excellent piece of villainy." Iago states: "devils . . . do suggest . . . As I do now." And each character says, in essentially the same way, that he is knowingly a dissembler. Aaron emphasizes his stratagem of burying gold under a tree as "cunningly" effected. Richard proclaims "nothing to back my suit at all/ But the plain Devil and dissembling looks." Iago states: "I am not what I am." Taken together, the three are the Vice-abstraction of the moralities suitably adapted to Elizabethan tastes and plots, identifying itself as Evil through Shakespearean soliloquy.

Character-revelation
(Psychological Soliloquy)

The word "character" is employed in the balance of this chapter, as in earlier sections of this work, principally to indicate character in the psychological dimension, not "character" meaning role in the play, member of the dramatis personae. That the revelation of character, in this sense, is one of the crowning glories of Shakespearean soliloquy goes almost without saying. The leading uses of character-revealing soliloquy, a category basically original with Shakespeare, are three. One is to demonstrate a persona's motivation. A second is to express intention. The third is to disclose and explain perturbation within the mind of the persona, reflecting the so-called "war within" (psychomachia) of the medieval English stage. There are certainly others, but the explorations here are limited rather strictly to these three categorizings of character soliloquy, again with the caution in mind that types of soliloquy are neither rigidly exclusive nor at all free from overlapping.

The first, and chronologically earliest (c. 1596, says Harrison), example of motivation-revealing soliloquy is the one delivered in *King John* by the Bastard Philip Faulconbridge, on having received his knighthood:

> A foot of honor better than I was,
> But many a many foot of land the worse.
> Well, now can I make any Joan a lady.
> "Good den, Sir Richard!" — "God-a-mercy, fellow!" —
> And if his name be George, I'll call him Peter,
> For new-made honor doth forget men's names.

> 'Tis too respective and too sociable
> For your conversion. Now your traveler,
> He and his toothpick at my Worship's mess,
> And when my knightly stomach is sufficed,
> Why then I suck my teeth and catechize
> My picked man of countries. "My dear sir,"
> Thus, leaning on mine elbow, I begin,
> "I shall beseech you" — that is Question now;
> And then comes Answer like an Absey book.
> "O sir," says Answer, "at your best command;
> At your employment; at your service, sir."
> "No, sir," says Question, "I, sweet sir, at yours."
> And so, ere Answer knows what Question would —
> Saving in dialogue of compliment,
> And talking of the Alps and Apennines,
> The Pyrenean and the River Po —
> It draws toward supper in conclusion so.
> But this is worshipful society
> And fits the mounting spirit like myself;
> For he is but a bastard to the time
> That doth not smack of observation.
> And so am I, whether I smack or no,
> And not alone in habit and device,
> Exterior form, outward accouterment,
> But from the inward motion to deliver
> Sweet, sweet, sweet poison for the age's tooth;
> Which, though I will not practice to deceive,
> Yet, to avoid deceit, I mean to learn,
> For it shall strew the footsteps of my rising.
>
> (I.i.182-216)

In the first twenty-three lines, Faulconbridge describes through the acerbity of mock dialogue that political guile ("dialogue of compliment") at once inevitable and to be avoided, which is so rampant in the "worshipful society" to which he has now been elevated. In the closing twelve lines, most pertinent here, he reveals that the exigencies of self-defense in his own position now prompt him to learn that guile for himself ("observation"), if not to practice it deliberately ("in habit and device"). Abounding in wordplay, as in the reflection from "picked" (193) back to "toothpick" (190), and the play on "bastard" which (207) derives from Philip's own illegitimacy, the soliloquy is nevertheless very direct in revealing his motive when at its close he states:

> Yet, to avoid deceit, I mean to learn,
> For it shall strew the footsteps of my rising.

A second Shakespearean soliloquy revealing motivation is that of Benedick ending Act II of *Much Ado*. In a sense, the author has the young Paduan unfolding his own character, within his announcement here that he is beginning to fall in love with Beatrice:

> Ha! "Against my will I am sent to bid you come in to dinner." There's a double meaning in that. "I took no more pains for those thanks than you took pains to thank me." That's as much as to say, "Any pains that I take for you is as easy as thanks." If I do not take pity of her, I am a villain; if I do not love her, I am a Jew. I will go get her picture. (II.iii.266-73)

To be sure, the reasons given by Benedick as prompting his suit for Beatrice's hand are silly rationalizations of the dinner message of Beatrice (which is repeated in Benedick's first two lines). His soliloquy is of course comic, and doubtless a light bit of satire on the tendency of young lovers to grasp at straws in feminine responses; his statement is couched as a facile moral justification to himself of his complete reversal of previous position. He is seizing on the most ordinary (and unfriendly) words of Beatrice as evidence of her attraction to him, an attraction not yet actually shown by the playwright. Nevertheless, the speech does display, if somewhat primitively within a framework of fairly early Shakespearean comedy (c. 1598), revelation of motivation within soliloquy, since real men may often be motivated in affairs of the heart by little more than is Benedick.

Harold S. Wilson's *On the Design of Shakespearian Tragedy* (Toronto: 1957), p. 126, finds Cressida revealing her motivation by means of soliloquy. "Cressida's real motives, amply suggested in her flippant parrying of her uncle Pandar's solicitations on Troilus's behalf, are explicitly stated for us in her soliloquy after Pandarus leaves her." Cressida's soliloquy follows:

> Words, vows, gifts, tears, and love's full sacrifice,
> He offers in another's enterprise.
> But more in Troilus thousandfold I see
> Than in the glass of Pandar's praise may be.
> Yet hold I off. Women are angels, wooing.
> Things won are done, joy's soul lies in the doing.
> That she beloved knows naught that knows not this —
> Men prize the thing ungained more than it is.
> That she was never yet that ever knew
> Love got so sweet as when desire did sue.
> Therefore this maxim out of love I teach:
> Achievement is command; ungained, beseech.
> Then though my heart's content firm love doth bear,
> Nothing of that shall from mine eyes appear.
>   (I.ii.308-21)

That Cressida intends to accept Troilus eventually, but to delay him at present, is apparent throughout the soliloquy: "Yet hold I off." Her motives for delaying him are also apparent, and as explicit: "Men prize the thing ungained more than it is." Cressida here is delivering a little homily to members of her sex, so doubtless the speech could be classified also as Minihomily, of a lighter sort. At any rate, she reveals that her wish to make herself even more desirable to the already impatient Troilus is her motive for withholding evidence of reciprocation yet a while. She is of course lauding anticipation over realization.

In *Antony and Cleopatra*, Enobarbus speaks a soliloquy which helps characterize him by laying bare his motives:

> I am alone the villain of the earth,
> And feel I am so most. O Antony,
> Thou mine of bounty, how wouldst thou have paid
> My better service when my turpitude
> Thou dost so crown with gold! This blows my heart.
> If swift thought break it not, a swifter mean
> Shall outstrike thought. But thought will do 't, I feel.
> I fight against thee! No, I will go seek
> Some ditch wherein to die, the foul'st best fits
> My latter part of life. (IV.v.30-39)

In this speech (briefly cited in an earlier instance) Enobarbus, lamenting his unworthiness, is thereby demonstrating an essential worth, candor to self. He is likewise displaying his motives for not joining the enemy to fight against Antony, despite having deserted his commander: it would be ignoble to oppose in combat a man who has so nobly sent after him his belongings and emoluments even in defection.

Within the initial scene of *Richard III*, Gloucester speaks two lesser known soliloquies which, among other services, express his intentions to the audience. Both exemplify the medieval Planning-speech, so called. They come from the playwright's earliest period when, as shown at some length in Chapter vi, medieval types of soliloquy (such as planning-speeches) most frequently appear. That they express intent is obvious: in fact, the word "intent" appears twice in the second speech. The soliloquies follow:

> Go tread the path that thou shalt ne'er return,
> Simple, plain Clarence! I do love thee so
> That I will shortly send thy soul to Heaven,
> If Heaven will take the present at our hands.
>
> (I.i.117-20)

(The speech is analyzed earlier in this chapter as example of homiletic self-exposure.) The second soliloquy of Richard reads:

> He [Hastings] cannot live, I hope, and must not die

> Till George be packed with post horse up to Heaven.
> I'll in, to urge his hatred more to Clarence,
> With lies well steeled with weighty arguments;
> And if I fail not in my deep intent,
> Clarence hath not another day to live.
> Which done, God take King Edward to His mercy,
> And leave the world for me to bustle in!
> For then I'll marry Warwick's youngest daughter.
> What though I killed her husband and her father?
> The readiest way to make the wench amends
> Is to become her husband and her father —
> The which will I, not all so much for love
> As for another secret close intent
> By marrying her which I must reach unto.
> But yet I run before my horse to market.
> Clarence still breathes, Edward still lives and reigns.
> When they are gone, then must I count my gains. (I.i.145-62)

In thus thoroughly delineating his plans for cruel actions (as though composing said plans while musing aloud), Gloucester is at the same time holding up to view his whole vicious nature.

The sixth soliloquy of Hamlet affords another example. It unveils his intent to put off slaying Claudius until a more propitious time, and details the reasons Hamlet has for so doing:

> Now might I do it pat, now he is praying,
> And now I'll do 't. And so he goes to Heaven,
> And so am I revenged. That would be scanned:
> A villain kills my father, and for that
> I, his sole son, do this same villain send
> To Heaven.
> Oh, this is hire and salary, not revenge.
> He took my father grossly, full of bread,
> With all his crimes broad blown, as flush as May,
> And how his audit stands who knows save Heaven?
> But in our circumstance and course of thought,
> 'Tis heavy with him. And am I then revenged,
> To take him in the purging of his soul,
> When he is fit and seasoned, for his passage?
> No.
> Up, sword, and know thou a more horrid hent.
> When he is drunk asleep, or in his rage,
> Or in the incestuous pleasure of his bed —
> At gaming, swearing, or about some act
> That has no relish of salvation in 't —
> Then trip him, that his heels may kick at Heaven

> And that his soul may be as damned and black
> As Hell, whereto it goes. My mother stays.
> This physic but prolongs thy sickly days. (III.iii.73-96)

This speech shows Hamlet in the very process of developing — of deciding on — his own intention ("Now might I do it . . ."). At the opening of the soliloquy, he has no sure resolve to announce to the audience ("That would be scanned"). By the end of the speech, he has announced intended action (i.e., delay: "Up, sword"). Whatever his reasons for delay, or however casuistic they may seem, his intent is revealed, if only a brand-new, just concluded intent.

Concluding instance of expression of intent is Hal's soliloquy ending the second scene of Act I in *I Henry IV*:

> I know you all, and will a while uphold
> The unyoked humor of your idleness.
> Yet herein will I imitate the sun,
> Who doth permit the base contagious clouds
> To smother up his beauty from the world,
> That, when he please again to be himself,
> Being wanted, he may be more wondered at
> By breaking through the foul and ugly mists
> Of vapors that did seem to strangle him.
> If all the year were playing holidays,
> To sport would be as tedious as to work.
> But when they seldom come, they wished-for come,
> And nothing pleaseth but rare accidents.
> So, when this loose behavior I throw off
> And pay the debt I never promisèd,
> By how much better than my word I am,
> By so much shall I falsify men's hopes.
> And like bright metal on a sullen ground,
> My reformation, glittering o'er my fault,
> Shall show more goodly and attract more eyes
> Than that which hath no foil to set it off.
> I'll so offend, to make offense a skill,
> Redeeming time when men think least I will.
> (I.ii.218-40)

While this declaration also reveals plot elements, as well as Hal's motives for staying with the Falstaff band "a while" longer, it most importantly informs in Hal's highly metaphorical affirmation ("Yet herein will I imitate the sun") that he knows just what he is doing in associating with the brigands — and just how he intends to turn that association to good use later on ("Redeeming time when men think least I will").

Interior-debate soliloquy openly reflects its medieval ancestry, the *Debat* of Good and Evil, originally staged with more than one persona visible on medieval platforms. The psychological subtleties to which Shakespeare eventually refined this "debate," however, distanced it forever from its simplistic form in the moralities.

In his early drama, interior-debate soliloquy is not necessarily far removed from its medieval origins. For instance, Launcelot Gobbo is seen in soliloquy debating with himself whether or not to run out on his master Shylock:

> Certainly my conscience will serve me to run from this Jew my master. The fiend is at mine elbow and tempts me, saying to me, "Gobbo, Launcelot Gobbo, good Launcelot," or "good Gobbo," or "good Launcelot Gobbo, use your legs, take the start, run away." My conscience says, "No, take heed, honest Launcelot, take heed, honest Gobbo," or, as aforesaid, "honest Launcelot Gobbo, do not run, scorn running with thy heels." Well, the most courageous fiend bids me pack. "Via!" says the fiend, "away!" says the fiend, "for the heavens, rouse up a brave mind," says the fiend, "and run." Well, my conscience, hanging about the neck of my heart, says very wisely to me, "My honest friend Launcelot, being an honest man's son" — or rather an honest woman's son, for indeed my father did something smack, something grow to, he had a kind of taste — well, my conscience says, "Launcelot, budge not." "Budge," says the fiend. "Budge not," says my conscience.
> . . . . (II.ii.1-19)

The medieval parentage of this soliloquy is readily perceivable; the piece exemplifies vestigial morality debate surviving in comic form. It is far distant from the mature diction and psychological subtlety of the Macbeth and Hamlet speeches quoted next in this section, although it certainly evinces linguistic subtlety. The clown identity of the speaker here is pointed up in the ludicrous amount of repetition of his own funny name ("Gobbo, Launcelot Gobbo, good Launcelot"), and in the run-on verbosity of his discourse. Such ludicrosity and wordiness relate it directly, if puckishly, to medieval soliloquy. In farcical tone and phrasing it reads, in fact, very much like the soliloquy of Mak cited from the mystery *The Second Shepherds' Play* in Chapter ii above. That the speaker is the Clown of the piece does not, however, negate the fact that there is a "war within," or that poor Launcelot Gobbo is frightened half out of his wits by the struggle. He resolves the debate in its closing lines, which are both hilarious and pathetic:

> The fiend gives the more friendly counsel. I will run, fiend, my heels are at your command. I will run. (II.ii.31-33)

Macbeth's first three soliloquies also display the "war within," although, as stated above, they are a far cry from the soliloquy of Launcelot Gobbo in sophistication of thought. Macbeth's first soliloquy runs thus (stage-directed in the text as a pair of asides but obviously bearing the status — and fore-stage positioning — of soliloquy):

> Two truths are told
> As happy prologues to the swelling act
> Of the imperial theme . . .
> This supernatural soliciting
> Cannot be ill, cannot be good. If ill,
> Why hath it given me earnest of success,
> Commencing in a truth? I am Thane of Cawdor.
> If good, why do I yield to that suggestion
> Whose horrid image doth unfix my hair
> And make my seated heart knock at my ribs,
> Against the use of nature? Present fears
> Are less than horrible imaginings.
> My thought, whose murder yet is but fantastical,
> Is smothered in surmise, and nothing is
> But what is not. (I.iii.127-42)

Here Macbeth, weighing the "two truths" in his mind, is a man patently at war with himself — and that is precisely what the audience is supposed to be shown by the soliloquy, character in dire turmoil ("and nothing is/ But what is not").

That Macbeth's second soliloquy ("If it were done" - I.vii.1-28) might too be labeled interior-debate is reinforced by William Rosen in *Shakespeare and the Craft of Tragedy* (Cambr., Mass.: 1960), p. 74, where Rosen affirms: "Unable to reason with his wife, who is obsessed with a single unquenchable purpose, Macbeth reasons and debates with himself; he becomes his own antagonist. His long soliloquy in Act I, scene vii, exposes to an audience a mind arguing with itself. Emphasizing not the attractions of murder, but the deterrents, Macbeth would talk himself into steadfast virtue." A few representative lines will point up Macbeth's inward battle:

> . . . we but teach
> Bloody instruction, which being taught return
> To plague the inventor. This even-handed justice
> Commends the ingredients of our poisoned chalice
> To our own lips.
> . . . .
> I have no spur
> To prick the sides of my intent, but only
> Vaulting ambition, which o'erleaps itself

And falls on the other. (I.vii.8-12, 25-28)

Macbeth's third soliloquy, one of the most arresting poetic passages in Shakespeare, also affords one of the most revelatory instancings of the "war within" a character. Calling to question the source of apparent evil is especially evident in one locution: "Or art thou but/ A dagger of the mind . . . ?" The soliloquy demands quotation in entirety in order that its basic (and brilliant) unity not be missed. No medieval soliloquy of Psychomachia approaches such psychological sophistication:

> Is this a dagger which I see before me,
> The handle toward my hand? Come, let me clutch thee.
> I have thee not, and yet I see thee still.
> Art thou not, fatal vision, sensible
> To feeling as to sight? Or art thou but
> A dagger of the mind, a false creation,
> Proceeding from the heat-oppressèd brain?
> I see thee yet, in form as palpable
> As this which now I draw.
> Thou marshal'st me the way that I was going,
> And such an instrument I was to use.
> Mine eyes are made the fools o' the other senses,
> Or else worth all the rest. I see thee still,
> And on thy blade and dudgeon gouts of blood
> Which was not so before. There's no such thing.
> It is the bloody business which informs
> Thus to mine eyes. Now o'er the one half-world
> Nature seems dead, and wicked dreams abuse
> The curtained sleep. Witchcraft celebrates
> Pale Hecate's offerings, and withered murder,
> Alarumed by his sentinel, the wolf,
> Whose howl's his watch, thus with his stealthy pace,
> With Tarquin's ravishing strides, toward his design
> Moves like a ghost. Thou sure and firm-set earth,
> Hear not my steps, which way they walk, for fear
> The very stones prate of my whereabout,
> And take the present horror from the time,
> Which now suits with it. Whiles I threat, he lives.
> Words to the heat of deeds too cold breath gives.
>   [A bell rings]
> I go, and it is done, The bell invites me.
> Hear it not, Duncan, for it is a knell
> That summons thee to Heaven, or to Hell.
>   (II.i.33-64)

The war within Macbeth here is that of the questioning of reality itself: "but a dagger of the mind," and again "There's no such thing," and "like a ghost." The speech is full of contraries, as in formal debate: a dagger — no such thing/ eyes the fools of senses — or else worth all the rest/ blood — which was not so before/ heat of deeds — cold breath. Further, there is in this soliloquy an insistence on setting off appearances against their potential reality, as in "Nature seems dead," and in all the "see" phrases, which also indicate Macbeth's need for reassurances concerning reality: "I see thee still," "I see thee yet," "I see thee still," "informs/ Thus to mine eyes."

The final examples of interior-debate are from *Hamlet*. H. D. F. Kitto has an observation pertinent here: "He [Hamlet] says: 'I have that within which passeth show;/ These but the trappings and the suits of woe.' What it is that he has within we learn from the first soliloquy, the depth and bitterness and despair of which are only diminished if we try to add to what he says conjectures of our own about disappointed ambition . . . now he has nothing to live for; the whole world 'is an unweed garden/ That grows to seed; things rank and gross in nature/ Possess it merely.'"[5] What Hamlet "has within" is a great and obvious confusion, a contention within his soul as to what has suddenly happened to his world. The negativism cited here by Kitto from the first soliloquy (I.ii.129-59) implies that there had once been another side to things, a positive outlook for Hamlet prior to the precipitative turn of events which has driven him now to such depths.

A glance at the most renowned soliloquy of all, Hamlet's fourth, concludes this chapter. To confirm a "war within" requires only a look at the opening line, the question analyzed, qualified and argued throughout all the remaining lines.

> To be, or not to be — that is the question.
>
> (III.i.56)

Hamlet, in the manner of formal forensics, has here put the question. He proceeds, still in the mode of public debate, to define and limit the question in the ensuing lines:

> Whether 'tis nobler in the mind to suffer
> The slings and arrows of outrageous fortune,
> Or to take arms against a sea of troubles
> And by opposing end them. (57-60)

He is still qualifying, and of course rhetorically replying to, the question at the end of the speech, a homily based on the "Scriptural text" of his own posed question:

> Thus conscience does make cowards of us all,
> And thus the native hue of resolution
> Is sicklied o'er with the pale cast of thought,
> And enterprises of great pitch and moment
> With this regard their currents turn awry

And lose the name of action. (83-88)

The speech is nothing if not internal debate.

Notes

Chapter IV

[1] Clemen, *Tragedy*, p. 51.

[2] *English Morality Plays and Moral Interludes*, p. 11. The two citations from *Castle of Perseverance* are from this source.

[3] Spivack, p. 46, terms these characters "repetition of a single stratagem."

[4] Manly, *Specimens*, I, 549. All quotations from Bale's *Kynge Johan* are from Manly, pp. 549-50.

[5] *Form and Meaning in Drama: A Study of Six Greek Plays and of Hamlet*, 2nd ed. (London: 1964), pp. 259-60.

Chapter V

Shakespearean: Structures and Language

In structure, whether Senecan orations, comic gibberish, or straightforward announcements, Shakespeare's soliloquies tend to resemble those from all eras. (The notorious exception is Plautus, whose intimacy and puckishness in addressing audiences [". . . if you will do me the kindness of listening"] have never been equaled.)

This chapter presents two detailed considerations. First, rather than renowned Shakespearean forms, it highlights two lesser known emotive types, "Passion" soliloquy and Lament. Both are essentially refinements on medieval modes, although Lament may be seen in diverse Shakespearean applications, and is therefore treated more fully. Second, through comparisons from throughout the canon, the chapter points up a surprising consistency of verbal artistry right from the early years, rather than a merely evolutionary improvement over the two decades.

A wholly separate structural question, Shakespeare's own important innovations in audience-address, is directed to the chapter following (vi).

Two Lesser Known Structures

First of the two structural categories, though not in any sort of primacy, is that of "Passion" soliloquy. Here is "announcement" by the speaker that he is the thrall of a single, overwhelming Passion, in the Elizabethan sense of that word, Anger, Grief, Jealousy, etc.[1] In this regard, Hamlet admonishes the players:

> Oh, it offends me to the soul to hear a robustious periwigpated fellow tear a passion to tatters, to very rags. (III.ii.8-11)

Leontes utters a speech in *The Winter's Tale* which exemplifies a "Passion"; it likewise reveals a portion of the plot of the piece. Leontes has just inquired as to the health of young Prince Mamillius, supposed living evidence of Queen Hermione's infidelity to Leontes:

> Fie, fie! No thought of him.
> The very thought of my revenges that way
> Recoil upon me. In himself too mighty,

> And in his parties, his alliance, let him be
> Unitl a time may serve. For present vengeance,
> Take it on her. Camillo and Polixenes
> Laugh at me, make their pastime at my sorrow.
> They should not laugh if I could reach them, nor
> Shall she within my power. (II.iii.18-26)

Leontes is enslaved by the Passion of Jealousy; his mutterings on vengeance toward persons absent and present suffice as indication of this. The two leading sub-elements of the speech are impatience and threat, prime ingredients of jealous rage.

Hamlet's second soliloquy limns a persona governed by the desire for vengeance. It is also the most — indeed, perhaps the only — decisive soliloquy of the Prince. The others tend to begin or close with conditional remarkings: "Oh, that this too too solid flesh would melt," "Now might I do it. . . ," or with self-beratings: "Oh, what a rogue and peasant slave am I!" But this one makes a promise, that he will not only remember but avenge his dead father:

> My tables — meet it is I set it down
> [Writing] That one may smile, and smile, and be a villain.
> At least I'm sure it may be so in Denmark.
> So, Uncle, there you are. Now to my word.
> It is "Adieu, adieu! Remember me."
> I have sworn 't. (I.v.107-12)

The demands of theatre per se, especially of the Elizabethan theatre with its emphasis on "Passion" speeches, cry out for a highly dramatic and gestural reply from Hamlet, and Shakespeare met those demands with a soliloquy memorably blunt and full of flourishes of hand ("I set it down," "there you are").

Berowne's hymning of love in *Love's Labor's Lost* concludes this brief treatment of Passion soliloquy. It is quite possible that the basic tone of his soliloquy should be interpreted as a kind of gentle mockery of Passion speeches, in view of the undercurrent of smiling scorn in such phrases as "sovereign of sighs and groans" — the piece is full of such "lord" metaphor. A few representative lines follow:

> And I, forsooth, in love! I, that have been love's whip —
> A very beadle to a humorous sigh,
> A critic, nay, a night-watch constable,
> A domineering pedant o'er the boy,
> Than whom no mortal so magnificent!
> This wimpled, whining, purblind, wayward boy,
> This senior-junior, giant-dwarf, Dan Cupid,
> Regent of love rhymes, lord of folded arms,

> The anointed sovereign of sighs and groans,
> Liege of all loiterers and malcontents,
> Dread prince of plackets, king of codpieces,
> Sole imperator and great general
> Of trotting 'paritors. — Oh, my little heart! —
> And I to be a corporal of his field,
> And wear his colors like a tumbler's hoop!
>
> (III.i.175-90)

The lines above amply illustrate that Berowne, formerly love's "whip" and "critic," is now a slave to that Passion.

Clemen devotes an entire chapter (xiv) to the Dramatic Lament and its forms, in his *English Tragedy Before Shakespeare*.[2] Clemen is primarily interested in showing, as on his p. 252, that Shakespeare's speeches of Dramatic Lament "take their direction from firmly established formulas laid down in the distant past." The present study is concerned with Shakespeare's use of specific traditional Lament modes in structuring soliloquies.

In his concentration on only a few forms of the Dramatic Lament used by Shakespeare, Clemen supplies among his few samples that of the formal apostrophe to grief or woe, and comments on it with originality as follows, on p. 238: ". . . the formal apostrophe to grief or woe must also have struck Shakespeare as altogether too rhetorical, and it is rarely found in his plays. In the string of apostrophes uttered by the grief-stricken Nurse at Juliet's death (*Romeo & Juliet*, IV.v.9ff.) it is quite obviously employed with the deliberate intention of laying on the colours too thickly. . . ."

Another such apostrophe is found in Act III of *Romeo*, where Juliet is elaborately bemoaning the hideous fact that it is the hand of Romeo that has slain her cousin Tybalt:

> O Nature, what hadst thou to do in Hell
> When thou didst bower the spirit of a fiend
> In mortal paradise of such sweet flesh?
> Was ever book containing such vile matter
> So fairly bound? Oh, that deceit should dwell
> In such a gorgeous palace! (III.ii.80-85)

This Lament, too, seems consciously elegant, like that of the Nurse quoted by Clemen, no doubt to contrast the more with the vernacularized, earthy sentiments of the Nurse ("Where's my man?") which follow it. Not in soliloquy, being addressed to the Nurse, it is offered here simply as another example of non-traditionalism in the use of Dramatic Lament by Shakespeare.

Titus Andronicus speaks what may be called his Lament to Grief, near the beginning of Act III. The stage directions specify that Titus "lieth down," in keeping with his opening metaphor of writing his sorrow in the dust.

> For these, Tribunes, in the dust I write
> My heart's deep languor and my soul's sad tears.
> Let my tears stanch the earth's dry appetite;
> My sons' sweet blood will make it shame and blush.
> O Earth, I will befriend thee more with rain
> That shall distil from these two ancient urns
> Than youthful April shall with all his showers.
> In summer's drought I'll drop upon thee still;
> In winter with warm tears I'll melt the snow,
> And keep eternal springtime on thy face,
> So thou refuse to drink my dear sons' blood.
>
> (III.i.12-22)

The brief soliloquy is almost entirely composed of metaphorical language lamenting Titus' grief: "my soul's sad tears," "refuse to drink my dear sons' blood." Within this context of what has been termed Shakespeare's worst-written tragedy, the highly Senecan Lament seems intended as traditional, unlike the two previous examples.

Another of the types of Lament in Shakespeare is the Prayer for Annihilation. Hamlet's first soliloquy may be categorized within the Annihilation-Prayer tradition, whether or not the author meant it as genuine death-longing or only as imprecatory musings of despair. In it the Prince prays

> Oh, that this too too solid flesh would melt,
> Thaw, and resolve itself into a dew!
>
> (I.ii.129-30)

Romeo utters a similar plea near the end of his soliloquy in the tomb, although it is more exactly termed apostrophe to Death and Its attendants. Like Juliet's Lament to her Nurse, this one is elegantly mannered, as is indeed the whole play.

> Eyes, look your last!
> Arms, take your last embrace! And lips, O you
> The doors of breath, seal with a righteous kiss
> A dateless bargain to engrossing death!
> Come, bitter conduct, come, unsavory guide!
> Thou desperate pilot, now at once run on
> The dashing rocks thy seasick weary bark.
>
> (V.iii.112-18)

Further examples of Prayer for Annihilation are in *Romeo* (III.ii.57-60) and in *Lear* (V.iii.312), where Juliet and Kent respectively pray for their hearts to break. Neither is in soliloquy.

In *III Henry VI*, Lord Clifford utters a long Lament, which also contains, not exceptionally, ingredients of plot-recapitulation and homily. Most essentially, though, the speech is a Death-lament, although Clifford, dying nobly, seems not so much lamenting his own demise as the numbers of needless deaths, including his, caused by the ineffectual rule of Henry. Clifford declares:

> Here burns my candle out. Aye, here it dies,
> Which, whiles it lasted, gave King Henry light.
> O Lancaster, I fear thy overthrow
> More than my body's parting with my soul!
> My love and fear glued many friends to thee,
> And, now I fall, thy tough commixture melts.
> Impairing Henry, strengthening misproud York,
> The common people swarm like summer flies,
> And whither fly the gnats but to the sun?
> And who shines now but Henry's enemies?
> O Phoebus, hadst thou never given consent
> That Phaethon should check thy fiery steeds,
> Thy burning car never had scorched the earth!
> And, Henry, hadst thou swayed as kings should do,
> Or as thy father and his father did,
> Giving no ground unto the House of York,
> They never then had sprung like summer flies,
> I and ten thousand in this luckless realm
> Had left no mourning widows for our death,
> And thou this day hadst kept thy chair in peace.
> . . . .
> (II.vi.1-20)

The candle image of the opening lines will be readily recognizable as a figure common to occasions of death in Shakespeare.

Finally, King Henry, in the same play, declaims a very long soliloquy opening the fifth scene of Act II. Depicted in Chapter vi as primitive soliloquy, it contains among other things a Lament bemoaning the cares incumbent on the crown. A portion of the speech follows:

> Oh, God! Methinks it were a happy life
> To be no better than a homely swain,
> To sit upon a hill, as I do now,
> To carve out dials quaintly, point by point,
> Thereby to see the minutes how they run —
> How many make the hour full complete,
> How many hours bring about the day,
> How many days will finish up the year,

> How many years a mortal man may live.
> When this is known, then to divide the times —
> So many hours must I tend my flock,
> So many hours must I take my rest,
> So many hours must I contemplate,
> So many hours must I sport myself;
> So many days my ewes have been with young,
> So many weeks ere the poor fools will ean,
> So many years ere I shall shear the fleece.
> So minutes, hours, days, months, and years,
> Passed over to the end they were created,
> Would bring white hairs unto a quiet grave.
> Ah, what a life were this! How sweet! How lovely!
> Gives not the hawthorn bush a sweeter shade
> To shepherds looking on their silly sheep
> Than doth a rich embroidered canopy
> To kings that fear their subjects' treachery?
> Oh, yes, it doth, a thousandfold it doth.
> And to conclude, the shepherd's homely curds,
> His cold thin drink out of his leather bottle,
> His wonted sleep under a fresh tree's shade,
> All which secure and sweetly he enjoys,
> Is far beyond a prince's delicates,
> His viands sparkling in a golden cup,
> His body couchèd in a curious bed,
> When care, mistrust, and treason waits on him.
>
> (II.v.21-54)

A more celebrated example of king's Lament soliloquy is that of Henry V (IV.i.247-301), too long and too well known to warrant full quotation here ("We must bear all. Oh, hard condition").

It is notable that all of the above examples of Lament soliloquy, excepting the one from *Hamlet*, are from pre-1600 plays. This is doubtless a representative proportion. In Chapter vi, on internal evolution in Shakespeare's soliloquies, the point is presented and amplified that overtly medieval traditions in soliloquy are far more likely to be reflected in his early works than in the later ones.

Language

It is commonly held that Shakespeare's soliloquies evolve in verbal refinement, exhibiting a progressive acquisition of technical skills, climaxing in mid-career and then dwindling into mostly lesser efforts toward the end. It is customary to assume that in *Hamlet, Othello,* or *Macbeth,* for example, soliloquy technique is measurably superior to that in the early plays, and certainly preferable to that of most of the late writings. But intensive review of three verse soliloquies, chosen to represent the finest from early, middle and final periods, demonstrates that assumptions of continuous technical growth are risky, in that irrespective of date of composition all three soliloquies display equal technical finesse, deftly devised and impeccably ordered, evocative of artlessness as only the highest art can be.

Since it is not practicable to study a great number of soliloquies exhaustively within a single chapter, the question must be approached intensively, rather than extensively. It has been divided here into four particulairzed searches: figurative language, alliteration, imagery per se, and word-play. Chronological range, limitation to verse, and more minute considerations insure that the three selected speeches afford legitimate elicitation of comparisons.

As Bernard Spivack says, the task of Shakespeare was to "stylize the soliloquy without impairing its integrity as private rumination."[3] To be sure, like other Elizabethan playwrights Shakespeare used the rhetorical commonplaces of the era as an aid in stylizing his soliloquies. John Gassner writes, in *Form and Idea in Modern Theatre*, probably reflecting the most prevalent current outlook: "Elizabethan drama provides striking examples of the opposite [i.e., opposite to realism] type of dramatic utterance — speech that is not realistically motivated. The writers of the Elizabethan and Jacobean ages favored rhetorical virtuosity either with or without dramatic motivation, and they also had acquired the habit of figurative writing from the over-use of analogy in philosophy and pseudo science."[4] "Rhetorical virtuosity" is doubtless one of the most frequent judgments made on Shakespearean soliloquies. In this chapter, however, the term "virtuosity" bears no pejorative connotations.

A soliloquy from *Romeo and Juliet*

Chronologically first of the three soliloquies, the epithalamium by Juliet opening the second scene of Act III is brilliantly illustrative of virtuosity in figurative language, as it is also replete with imagery per se, alliteration, and word-play, the four main areas of concern in this study.

>   Gallop apace, you fiery-footed steeds,
>   Toward Phoebus' lodging. Such a wagoner
>   As Phaeton would whip you to the west,
>   And bring in cloudy night immediately.
>   Spread thy close curtain, love-performing night,
>   That runaways' eyes may wink, and Romeo
>   Leap to these arms, untalked of and unseen.
>   Lovers can see to do their amorous rites
>   By their own beauties; or, if love be blind,
>   It best agrees with night. Come, civil night,
>   Thou sober-suited matron, all in black,

> And learn me how to lose a winning match
> Played for a pair of stainless maidenhoods.
> Hood my unmanned blood bating in my cheeks
> With thy black mantle, till strange love grown bold
> Think true love acted simple modesty.
> Come, night, come, Romeo, come, thou day in night,
> For thou wilt lie upon the wings of night
> Whiter than new snow on a raven's back.
> Come, gentle night, come, loving, black-browed night,
> Give me my Romeo; and when he shall die,
> Take him and cut him out in little stars,
> And he will lmake the face of heaven so fine
> That all the world will be in love with night,
> And pay no worship to the garish sun.
> Oh, I have bought the mansion of a love,
> But not possessed it, and though I am sold,
> Not yet enjoyed. So tedious is this day
> As is the night before some festival
> To an impatient child that hath new robes
>   And may not wear them. (III.ii.1-30)

This soliloquy is eminently characteristic of the earlier Shakespeare: it is a commonplace of criticism to note the artistic verbosity and constant lyricizing of daily events within his early plays. Juliet's song is also extremely technical, in repleteness of figurative device, variety of imagery, and abundance of plays on words.

 As for the figures of speech in Juliet's song, the poem is first of all one long apostrophe. Daytime is apostrophized in its opening lines ("you fiery-footed steeds"), and then, in a skillful transition between poetic contraries, the author brings on via line 4 his *invocatio* to night in line 5 ("Spread thy close curtain, love-performing night"), the major apostrophe of the poem and the one bestowing handsome unity by its unrelenting continuation throughout the soliloquy. (There is controversy about the identity of the "runaways" of line 6 [the sun, or night?]; the reference seems clearly to Phoebus, given the associativeness of runaways and steeds.) Civil [that is, respectable] night is again apostrophized in line 10, described in line 11, and urged in lines 12-16 to act favorably toward the speaker. Strange (unfamiliar) love is contrasted to love enacted, in lines 15 and 16 ("strange love . . . true love"), in one of the song's several instances of polarity. The final apostrophe is in the long address to night occupying lines 17-25 ("Come, gentle night").

 Virtuosity in figurativeness does not stop with apostrophizing. The rush of contraries in the poem, two of them (day-night, strange love-true love) already emphasized, furnish a soliloquy which is not only one long apostrophe but also one practically continuous listing of opposites. Within the single major and unmistakable opposing of day to night lie the several polarities constituting it. There are — to count only the obvious contraries — fiery-cloudy, losing-winning, eyes-unseen, light-black, bold-modest, day-in-night (Romeo), snow-raven, night's fine face-garish sun, bought-sold, bought-not possessed.

Virtuosity reappears in the amount of alliteration. Gallo*p* a*p*ace, *f*iery-*f*ooted, the "t's" in foo*t*ed s*t*eeds/ *T*oward, as well as *w*agoner *w*ould *w*hip *w*est, and *c*lose *c*urtain, all come within the first five lines, and many, many more instances throughout the poem, except for such skillful ones as in amo*r*ous *r*ites, or wi*l*t *l*ie and ne*w* sno*w*, are omitted for the sake of brevity.

The great number of adjectives is also worthy of mention, including the rather typically Elizabethan technique of the compound adjective, "love-performing," "black-browed."

Imagery per se is richly evident and notable in Juliet's song. A high variety is engendered by the choices ranging from fire and horsemanship to clouds and blindness, all within the first nine lines. Games are soon after involved in the speech, and falconry, too, in lines 12-15. In line 25 appears the imagery of worship, as in lines 26-28 a financial metaphor (bought-sold)." (Cf. Sonnets 30, 67, and 146, with their fiscal conceits.) Perhaps, indeed, the principal reason for the memorableness of the imagery in Shakespearean soliloquy — aside from its inestimable appropriateness — is its almost endless variety and range.

Finally, as to word-play, a quibble on maidenheads may exist in "unmanned blood" in line 14, stressing the idea of Juliet's virgin state. In line 28 "enjoyed" has a double meaning, surely, of both sexual fulfillment and financial metaphor. Given the tendency of Shakespeare to punning, "beauties" in line 9 may also bear a hidden meaning, that of pretty damsels, by (that is, with) whom lovers do their amorous rites. And the "sober-suited matron" of line 11 might well be the matron whose suitors approach her soberly in muttering their suits of love. It was Dr. Johnson who, in the Dictionary of 1755, defined the punster as "a quibble; a low wit who endeavours at reputation by double meaning,"[5] but his opinion that "a quibble is the golden apple for which he [Shakespeare] will always turn aside"[6] has probably been in this day turned aside itself by the ever growing respect for Shakespeare's way with word-play. Molly Mahood's work, *Shakespeare's Wordplay* (London: 1957), pp. 20-21, presents what is doubtless the current, favorable estimate or "defense" of Shakespeare's playing with words: "Shakespeare plays with verbal meanings, not because the rhetoricians approve of wordplay, but because his imagination as a poet works through puns, or because his characters are placed in situations where puns help to clarify the particular view of life that he seeks to present in a particular play."

A Soliloquy from *Hamlet*

The second soliloquy of the three chosen for intensive review in this chapter is without doubt the most oft repeated (in part, at least) in all literature, Hamlet's fourth, "To be, or not to be." This choice falls approximately midway within the author's career as dramatist, or within the "Balanced" period of the four postulated by Harrison to delineate Shakespeare's output: "Early, Balanced, Overflowing, and Final."[7] Juliet's "Day-Night" soliloquy above represents what is universally regarded as the "Early" Shakespeare. Hamlet's speech follows:

> To be, or not to be — that is the question.
> Whether 'tis nobler in the mind to suffer
> The slings and arrows of outrageous fortune,
> Or to take arms against a sea of troubles
> And by opposing end them. To die, to sleep —
> No more, and by a sleep to say we end
> The heartache and the thousand natural shocks
> That flesh is heir to. 'Tis a consummation
> Devoutly to be wished. To die, to sleep,
> To sleep — perchance to dream. Aye, there's the rub,
> For in that sleep of death what dreams may come
> When we have shuffled off this mortal coil
> Must give us pause. There's the respect
> That makes calamity of so long life.
> For who would bear the whips and scorns of time,
> The oppressor's wrong, the proud man's contumely,
> The pangs of dèspised love, the law's delay,
> The insolence of office and the spurns
> That patient merit of the unworthy takes,
> When he himself might his quietus make
> With a bare bodkin? Who would fardels bear,
> To grunt and sweat under a weary life,
> But that the dread of something after death,
> The undiscovered country from whose bourn
> No traveler returns, puzzles the will,
> And makes us rather bear those ills we have
> Than fly to others that we know not of?
> Thus conscience does make cowards of us all,
> And thus the native hue of resolution
> Is sicklied o'er with the pale cast of thought,
> And enterprises of great pitch and moment
> With this regard their currents turn awry
> And lose the name of action. (III.i.56-88)

Of the four concerns, figurative device, imagery, alliteration and word-play, there is no less in this speech than the wealth found in Juliet's epithalamium. The initial figure is a military one, slings, arrows, taking arms, opposing. The second involves the equation of death to sleep, and includes the best known death-wish in literature, "a consummation devoutly to be wished," as well as a "rub" disrupting the desire for the sleep-solace of dying. In the Juliet speech the ruling figure was apostrophe; in Hamlet's it is simile: important to this study is not the contrast in types of metaphor but the likeness in the great amount of metaphorical language, and, within each soliloquy, the consistency of whatever metaphorical types are used.

To continue with examination of Hamlet's metaphors, the figure of being whipped is succeeded by scorns, oppressions, contumely, pangs, delay, insolence and spurnings, a congruence of metaphor exemplified by the profusion of similar hurts (stylistically reminiscent of the flood of contraries in Juliet's soliloquy).

Lines 76-82 are echoed somewhat in Claudio's speech to his sister Isabella in *Measure* (III.i.118-32), thought to have been written at about the same time as *Hamlet* (c. 1604 and c. 1600 respectively).[8] Claudio says:

> Aye, but to die, and go we know not where,
> To lie in cold obstruction and to rot,
> . . . .
> The weariest and most loathèd worldly life
> That age, ache, penury, and imprisonment
> Can lay on nature is a paradise
> To what we fear of death. (III.i.118-32)

In line 79 Hamlet's simile is that of death and undiscovered country, as he continues the enumeration of burdens ("Fardels," "those ills we have," "others we know not of"). Then comes the famed prosopopoeia of conscience, enabled to "make cowards of us all," and the memorable color-simile — specially applied in descriptions of Hamlet himself by nineteenth-century German and English Romantics — of resolution as being sicklied o'er with alien hue, "the pale cast of thought." Finally, enterprises are also given a sort of embodiment, and they too are seen susceptible to skewed turnings and vanished identities.

A full stream of alliteration was visible in Juliet's soliloquy. There is an equal flow in Hamlet's. More obvious instances include *s*uffer-*s*lings, *t*o *t*ake and *a*rms *a*gainst *a* (both in the same line), *s*leep-*s*ay, and probably the *sh* in *sh*ocks and fl*e*sh of adjoining lines, supplemented by the same sibilance in wi*sh*ed in the following line. The alliteration resident in constant repetition of infinitives creates the dominant locution of the first part of this soliloquy, with *to* be-*to* be, *to* suffer, *to* take and *[to]* end, *to* die, *to* sleep (repeated verbatim four lines later), *to* say, a third use of *to* sleep (in *To* die, *to* sleep,/ *To* sleep . . .), and finally *to* dream. Notable too is the provision of alliterative transition between sentences in "heir *to*. *'Tis*," as well as later in the "*p*'s" in o*p*pressor's wrong, the *p*roud man's contumely/ The *p*angs of dès*p*ised love, and further into s*p*urns, *p*atient. The more simple alliterating continues in such phrases as *l*ong *l*ife, or, in line 75, the elementary alliteration in *h*e *h*imself might *h*is. This soliloquy is fully as alliterative as that of Juliet written in the author's early career, reinforcing the finding of this study that the language of Shakespearean soliloquy is essentially consistent in technique throughout the canon.

Hamlet's soliloquy is also at least as much based on poetic contraries as was that of Juliet. Indeed, the prime mover of the speech is its polarization of life and death right in the opening line, "To be, or not to be." As the writer specified, "that is the question." And the entire utterance arrays opposites together, to suffer or to take arms, to bear the fardels or to make quietus with a bodkin, to prefer the ills we have over those we know not of, resolution sicklied, enterprises awry. Here again Shakespeare is using techniques of figurative language like, or remarkably similar to, those in his early soliloquy for Juliet.

While there is in Hamlet's speech some repetition of images from the Juliet soliloquy (whips, terms from falconry, and of course the image of dying), the subject-matter of the two is so very different that comparison of imagery is not really feasible. But a point made concerning the soliloquy of Juliet applies equally to Hamlet's: there is an unutterable variety and range of imagery in it, from taking arms and sweating to sleeping, with color-imagery, travel, and oceans all somewhere in between. Certainly, however, Hamlet's images are plain and exact, rather than beautiful and romantic like Juliet's.

Word-play in Hamlet's famed fourth is not the same as in the Juliet speech. In the latter is a considerable number of puns. In Hamlet's soliloquy there is also a very definite playing with words — but it should perhaps be called working with them, since the word-play is by no means playful, as it sometimes is for Juliet. Rather, it is the balancing of phrases, a back-and-forth, swinging rhythm of opposites arrayed and infinitives repeated, which constitutes the word-play in Hamlet's oration. Perhaps there is a more mature technician of poetry at work in this type of word-play, but not necessarily a "better" or more effective one than in the earlier soliloquy. This question is dealt with in detail at the conclusion of this chapter, following the perusal of the Caliban soliloquy from late in the career.

A Soliloquy from *The Tempest*

The third and last soliloquy chosen to be scrutinized for language is that of Caliban from Act II, Scene ii of *The Tempest*, in order, as previously indicated, to encompass some chronological perspective on Shakespearean soliloquy by moving from one in *Romeo* to one in *Hamlet*, and concluding with one from the end of the canon, from what was probably the last independently written play. Caliban's, like those of Juliet and Hamlet, is a highly figurative speech. The controlling conceit is the nature of the abuses heaped by Prospero on his crude serving-man. Despite the relative brevity of the speech (14 lines, as compared to 30 for the Juliet speech and 33 for Hamlet's), it is full of metaphor and images, and entirely dependent on a particular figurative device, as the soliloquies of Juliet and Hamlet were respectively dependent mainly on apostrophe and simile. The device dominating Caliban's soliloquy is hyperbole, the hyperbole of magic which furnishes the governing metaphor and imagery of the whole play, as well as the exaggerations in Caliban's mind, near to madness if not already in dementia. The speech is even accompanied by hyperbolic stage effects ("A noise of thunder heard"). The soliloquy follows:

> All the infections that the sun sucks up
> From bogs, fens, flats, on Prosper fall, and make him
> By inchmeal a disease! His spirits hear me,
> And yet I needs must curse. But they'll nor pinch,
> Fright me with urchin shows, pitch me i' the mire,
> Nor lead me, like a firebrand, in the dark
> Out of my way, unless he bid 'em. But
> For every trifle are they set upon me —
> Sometime like apes, that mow and chatter at me,
> And after bite me; then like hedgehogs, which
> Lie tumbling in my barefoot way and mount
> Their pricks at my footfall. Sometime am I
> All wound with adders, who with cloven tongues
> Do hiss me into madness. (II.ii.1-14)

The speech begins with an imprecation invoking disease ("infections") on the head of Caliban's abuser. Cursing is in itself most often hyperbolic, most usually formed as a wish. Caliban's wish is that Prospero be overcome by an onslaught of fenny infections. Notable is the repetition of topographical features in "bogs, fens, flats," a triad exemplifying hyperbole, the hyperbole of lost, fearsome places overlain with unreasoned connotations of frightful bogeys. It is fitting, and probably not mere coincidence, by the way, that the character who is himself termed "monster" in Trinculo's soliloquy (II.ii.31) should utter images of monstrosity.

The word "fright," in line 5, sets the tone of the speech, a note of fear, Caliban's fear of being overheard, his fear of constant, invisible visitation by the omnipotent spirits of Prospero. "Fright," "set upon me," "bite me," "hiss," all are terms of fearsome condition, of the exaggerated apprehensiveness all humans feel when confronted by untraversed, unknown places, "undiscovered countries." Caliban's verbs and verb phrases aptly connote such places as bogs, fens, flats, promoting, in their entire appropriateness, the tone of Caliban's exaggerative reaction to his fears.

Caliban's near-madness is probably seen substantiated in his own words, at the end of the soliloquy, where he speaks of

> adders, who with cloven tongues
> Do hiss me into madness. (11. 13-14)

Madness, whatever its form, is a hyperbole, a larger-than-life state. As often as not it involves the afflicted's hyperbolizing of very ordinary fears which are not longer recognized as such. Given the importance of magic to the plot, there can be no certainty as to whether Shakespeare was painting Caliban in delirium via such fearsome metaphors. In fact, the question is perhaps mainly whether the animal and reptile names are meant as metaphors for Caliban's tremors or meant to be taken "literally" as agents of Prospero's magical powers. Whatever the authorial intent, the names remain, and they constitute a menacing bestiary, not of familiar, domestic animals but of wild, potentially harmful creatures: apes, hedgehogs (harmful to bare feet, if not otherwise dangerous!), adders. And they are active beasts, whether in Caliban's delirious imaginings or in his actual path: chattering apes who grimace and bite, tumbling, quill-sticking porcupines, hissing, man-encoiling adders. Either way, imagined or real, they create the exaggerated effect obviously desired by the playwright for Caliban's plight, and constitute the soliloquy's governing figurative device, hyperbole.

Shakespeare cultivates contraries in Caliban's soliloquy nearly as much as in those of Juliet and Hamlet. The speech is only approximately half as long as each of the other two, so it is not possible to compare directly as to quantity of contraries in the poetry. Sun is opposed to bogs in the opening lines, as is the sun's evaporation to infections falling on Prospero. (Note the up-down polarity of evaporation vs. falling as well as the contrasting of healthful sun vs. infection.) In the next two lines the dangers of cursing are opposed to Caliban's need to curse. Firebrand and dark are as opposite as their concomitants, the known (signified by the verb "lead") and the unknown ("out of my way"), as too are goblin shows and mire (the flashing eyes, i.e., light, of goblin shows and the mud, i.e., dark, or mire). In addition, the mowing and chattering of apes is a contrary to the quiet tumbling and quill-pointing of hedgehogs,, as for that matter are the hedgehogs' pricks to bare feet. The entire declamation is based on primary opposites, all-powerful Prospero, the master, vs. helpless Caliban, the slave. And, finally, it features two important "but's" which indicate conditions of opposition (confrontation): "But . . . unless he bid 'em," and "But/ For every trifle are they set upon me."

As in the previous two soliloquies considered in this review, Juliet's and Hamlet's, alliteration is a streaming force in the rhetoric. Noteworthy is the carry-over alliteration from in*fe*ctions in the initial line to *fe*ns, and *f*lats in the second. And within the second line, the author offers *f*ens, *f*lats, *f*all, subsequent of course to *s*un *s*ucks in the first. The same technique of carried-over sounds shows in *m*ake and inch*m*eal of the second and third lines. In later lines are *h*is and *h*ear, need*s* mu*s*t cur*s*e (a very emphatic repetition of sibilance), followed by *p*inch and *p*itch (another carry-over between lines), *b*id and *b*ut, *s*et and *s*ometime and ape*s* (another, rather delicate, sibilance), and so on through bare*f*oot and *f*oot*f*all, hi*ss* and madne*ss*.

In further parallel to the soliloquies from Juliet and Hamlet, this one contains a great variety of imagery. Much of it, the names of animals, etc., has already been emphasized as contraries. Other images heightening the hyperbole of the passage include goblins ("urchin shows"), mire, and firebrand in the dark (leading Caliban out of his way). Variety and range in imagery are easily apparent, from bogs to sun, apes to hedgehogs.

Word-play in Caliban's soliloquy is mainly a question of balancings of phrase, more as in Hamlet's soliloquy than as in Juliet's. There are two kinds of balancing in this speech, the positive-negative weighing of contraries treated earlier and the counter-poising of parallel clauses within individual sentences. The two types of word-play go together. For example, the sentence

>   His spirits hear me,
> And yet I needs must curse. (11. 3-4)

offers a vis-à-vis of negative and positive ideas, within the equilibrium inherent in a compound sentence, exemplifying the antithetic parallelism so common in the contemporaneous King James Scriptures. The next lines (4-7) rely on the parallelism of a compound predicate (a series of main verbs: pinch, fright, pitch, lead), skillful word-play, certainly. Lines 8-12 rely on the equation of two adverbial prepositional phrases ("like apes," "like hedgehogs"), which themselves introduce parallelled adjective clauses ("that mow and chatter at me,/ And after bite me" and "which lie tumbling . . . and mount"), followed immediately by another sentence (11. 12-14) which contains a similarly structured adjective clause ("who with cloven tongues/ Do hiss me"). This is word-play in its most clever degree. The speech is above all dependent on its verbs, both for compounding its tone of fear and for introducing its variety of imagery.

To state briefly the findings of this chapter, based on no preconceptions and consequently something of a surprise to the writer, it is clear that the techniques of language in Shakespeare's best soliloquies remain essentially the same throughout his playwriting career. Three acclaimed verse soliloquies were selected for scrutiny, from three plays chronologically distributed through the canon. These three speeches, the Night-Day oration by Juliet (III.ii.1-30), Hamlet's "To be" soliloquy (III.i.56-88), and Caliban's plaint on Prospero's abuses (II.ii.1-14), reveal among them remarkable parallelisms in (1) a single or main figurative device governing each soliloquy, (2) extreme dependence on alliteration, (3) command of an uncountable variety of images, and (4) consummate fluency with word ordering, sentence structure, and balancing of grammatical elements, colligated here as word-play. To be sure, Shakespeare did intend and achieve, in works of his middle and late career, a heightened spontaneity of speaking (exemplified in Hamlet's fourth soliloquy reviewed here). He also selected different kinds of imagery — not different amounts — for the soliloquies of his maturer years, as his plot interests changed from chronicle plays and stories of young love to stark tragedies or tales of familial reconciliation. He was by then writing soliloquies somewhat different in content from earlier ones, but showing in his craft not so much improvement as alteration. The differences in context and techniques are detailed in the next chapter, dealing with evolutionary factors within Shakespearean soliloquy. There the primitivism seen on occasion in his earliest soliloquies is also reviewed.

Notes

Chapter V

[1] For a thorough treatment of Elizabethan faculty psychology of the "Passions" see Lily B. Campbell, *Shakespeare's Tragic Heroes: Slaves of Passion* (New York: 1930), passim, and especially Section II, "Moral Philosophy in Shakespeare's Day."

[2] Trans. T. S. Dorsch (London: 1961).

[3] *Shakespeare and the Allegory of Evil* (New York: 1958), p. 42.

[4] (New York: 1956), pp. 38-39.

[5] E. L. McAdam, Jr., and George Milne, *Johnson's Dictionary* (New York: 1963), p. 321.

[6] *The Literature of England*, eds. George K. Anderson and Wm. E. Buckler, 5th ed. (Glenview, Ill.: 1966), I, 1639.

[7] Harrison, p. 67.

[8] Harrison, pp. 1100 and 881, respectively.

Chapter VI

Shakespearean: Evolution Within

Successive portions of this study have traced an evolution of English soliloquy from origins in pre-classical dramatic literature through classical Greek and Roman traditions and on through medieval English drama. This final chapter treats of evolution within Shakespearean soliloquy itself.

Such evolution is most readily apparent in the extreme variations of refinement between a number of declamations in Shakespeare's earliest history plays and the justly renowned orations of his later tragedies. Primitiveness is undeniably resident in numerous speeches from the histories presumed to have been written within the first five or six years of his career. The greatest incidence of sophistication occurs in tragedy soliloquy of the later fifteen years or so, as in *Julius Caesar, Hamlet, King Lear,* and *Macbeth.*

"Primitiveness" and "sophistication" are, for the present context, merely terms of convenience. No single soliloquy of Shakespeare is entirely free from either aspect, and both early and late soliloquies display nearly equal proportions of each. (Such a speech is quoted on the pages immediately following.) Also, as asserted in the previous chapter, the balance is weighted toward demonstrable polish and poise throughout the plays.

The judgment of primitiveness, within the confines of this chapter, is partly based on heavy dependence on soliloquy conventions, that is, on medieval types of set speech, and on posturings reminiscent of Senecan heroes. It also comprises extravagances in language, such as elaborate conceits, catachresis, the veritable piling-on of images, and occasional floods of Senecan rhetoric. Sophistication in Shakespearean soliloquy, on the other hand, denotes originality of structure and diction, i.e., virtual abandonment of medieval forms of set speech, much less rigid adherence in verse to strictures of rhythm for the sake of rhythm (in Granville-Barker's words, tending "to loosen and even break down the form of the verse"),[1] and ever so much less dependence on elaborately figurative language. Sophistication is also exemplified by much more emphasis on approximating the rhythms and diction of natural, or spontaneous, speaking, as opposed to the unrelenting rhythms and stilted utterance derived from pre-Shakespearean set speech.

A speech illustrating a fairly even mixture of both primitiveness and refinement in Shakespearean soliloquy is that spoken by Richard, Duke of Gloucester, at the close of Scene ii in Act III of *III Henry VI*, surely one of the author's longest soliloquies:

> Aye, Edward will use women honorably.
> Would he were wasted, marrow, bones and all,
> That from his loins no hopeful branch may spring
> To cross me from the golden time I look for!
> And yet, between my soul's desire and me —
> The lustful Edward's title buried —
> Is Clarence, Henry, and his son young Edward,
> And all the unlooked for issue of their bodies,
> To take their rooms, ere I can place myself.
> A cold premeditation for my purpose!
> Why, then, I do but dream on sovereignty,
> Like one that stands upon a promontory
> And spies a far-off shore where he would tread,
> Wishing his foot were equal with his eye,
> And chides the sea that sunders him from thence,
> Saying he'll lade it dry to have his way:
> So do I wish the crown, being so far off,
> And so I chide the means that keeps me from it,
> And so I say I'll cut the causes off,
> Flattering me with impossibilities.
> My eye's too quick, my heart o'erweens too much,
> Unless my hand and strength could equal them.
> Well, say there is no kingdom then for Richard.
> What other pleasure can the world afford?
> I'll make my heaven in a lady's lap,
> And deck my body in gay ornaments,
> And witch sweet ladies with my words and looks.
> Oh, miserable thought, and more unlikely
> Than to accomplish twenty golden crowns!
> Why, love forswore me in my mother's womb
> And, for I should not deal in her soft laws,
> She did corrupt frail nature with some bribe
> To shrink mine arm up like a withered shrub,
> To make an envious mountain on my back,
> Where sits deformity to mock my body,
> To shape my legs of an unequal size,
> To disproportion me in every part,
> Like to a chaos, or an unlicked bear whelp
> That carries no impression like the dam.
> And am I then a man to be beloved?
> Oh, monstrous fault, to harbor such a thought!
> Then, since this earth affords no joy to me

> But to command, to check, to o'erbear such
> As are of better person than myself,
> I'll make my heaven to dream upon the crown
> And, whiles I live, to account this world but Hell
> Until my misshaped trunk that bears this head
> Be round impalèd with a glorious crown.
> And yet I know not how to get the crown,
> For many lives stand between me and home.
> And I — like one lost in a thorny wood,
> That rends the thorns and is rent with the thorns,
> Seeking a way and straying from the way,
> Not knowing how to find the open air,
> But toiling desperately to find it out —
> Torment myself to catch the English crown.
> And from that torment I will free myself,
> Or hew my way out with a bloody ax.
> Why, I can smile, and murder whiles I smile,
> And cry "Content" to that which grieves my heart,
> And wet my cheeks with artificial tears,
> And frame my face to all occasions.
> I'll drown more sailors than the mermaid shall;
> I'll slay more gazers than the basilisk;
> I'll play the orator as well as Nestor,
> Deceive more slyly than Ulysses could,
> And, like a Sinon, take another Troy.
> I can add colors to the chameleon,
> Change shapes with Proteus for advantages,
> And set the murderous Machiavel to school.
> Can I do this, and cannot get a crown?
> Tut, were it farther off, I'll pluck it down.
>
> (III.ii.124-95)

Collaborative effort or not ("the case cannot be proved either way," says Harrison, p. 105), this play is representative of the very earliest work of Shakespeare. Harrison dates it as c. 1592. Mahood states, p. 28, that the speech is "decked out with rhetorical figures of words, learnt from Marlowe and others," but, she adds, "its deeper organisation is like that of the verse in any of Shakespeare's better authenticated plays." Gloucester's soliloquy contains elements of both the primitiveness usually associated with the earlier plays and the sophistication ordinarily expected (but not always found) in Shakespeare's later dramas. In short, it is a mixture, neither thoroughly primitive nor memorably polished.

The most visible evidence of primitiveness in the speech is doubtless its concluding passage of classical allusions (basilisk, Ulysses, Proteus — 11. 186-93). This piling-on of mythical and legendary references (and a single historical one, "Machiavel") reads more like an appendix than like an integral part of the soliloquy. However, this single passage is not the only evidence of primitiveness. Somewhat less overt extravagance appears in lines 135-39 where an elaborate string of verbs and verbals — eight, in fact — is appended to the subject-pronoun "one" to make the intricate promontory simile ("stands," "spies," "tread," "Wishing," "chides," "Saying," "lade," "to have"). And in lines 140-42 directly following, the four-fold use of "so" fails its intended emphasis by calling undue attention to the word itself. In over-all effect, this is a conventional set speech, resembling Resolution-speeches of pre-Shakespearean drama more than, say, the subtle musings of a Macbeth or Hamlet.

On the other hand, elements of sophistication are quite evident in Richard's soliloquy. A single metaphor ("how to get the crown") pervades and dominates the piece, thoroughly unifying it in spite of its closing catalogue of classical allusions; the metaphor is visible in lines 127 ("the golden time"), 134-45 ("I wish the crown"), 152 ("twenty golden crowns"), and throughout lines 165-85. This latter (165-85) is a powerful passage of mature, eminently readable (or "listenable") soliloquy ("to dream upon the crown"), if not quite demonstrating the spontaneity of language found in some of the later plays. Originality of diction is apparent not only in this central section of the speech but also in lines 146-52: words can hardly be more direct than "I'll make my heaven in a lady's lap." And in lines 140-42, criticized above for primitive repetition of "so," poetic skill does surface in repeating the concepts of "wish" and "chide" from the lines immediately previous, as also in the alliterating of sibilants in *s*o I *s*ay . . . cau*s*es. In fact, skillful alliteration is one of the strong points of this speech, as in lines 136-39, which also include, by the way, much use of sibilant sound (*s*pies . . . *s*hore *w*here he *w*ould tread,/ *W*ishing his foot *w*ere equal *w*ith his eye — also the "w" sound in eq*u*al — chide*s* the *s*ea that *s*under*s* him from then*c*e,/ *S*aying). In fine, the soliloquy is a combination of primitiveness and sophistication, with probably a slight edge in favor of the latter.

Early Primitiveness

A number of soliloquies in early plays of Shakespeare reflect his dependence on a medieval form of soliloquy labeled by Clemen in *English Tragedy Before Shakespeare* as "Resolution-speeches."[2] In the fourth act of *King John* (dated by Harrison as c. 1596) the child Arthur speaks such a "Resolution-speech," informing the audience of his resolve to leap from the wall and escape his captors:

> The wall is high, and yet will I leap down.
> Good ground, be pitiful and hurt me not!
> There's few or none do know me. If they did,
> This shipboy's semblance hath disguised me quite.
> I am afraid; and yet I'll venture it.

> If I get down, and do not break my limbs,
> I'll find a thousand shifts to get away.
> As good to die and go, as die and stay.
> Oh, me! My uncle's spirit is in these stones.
> Heaven take my soul, and England keep my bones!
> (IV.iii.1-10)

Such soliloquy labors the obvious, to judge it even by most Elizabethan stage standards, let alone those of the present Age of Naturalism.

Another Resolution-speech is that by York in Act III (i.331-83) of *II Henry VI*, of which the opening six lines are quoted here:

> Now, York, or never, steel thy fearful thoughts
> And change misdoubt to resolution.
> Be that thou hopest to be, or what thou art
> Resign to death; it is not worth the enjoying.
> Let pale-faced fear keep with the mean-born man
> And find no harbor in a royal heart.

Other examples of Shakespeare's reliance on this medieval soliloquy convention exist in the early plays, as in the brief soliloquy serving also to identify Iden as a "good guy" in Act IV of the same play:

> Lord, who would live turmoilèd in the Court,
> And may enjoy such quiet walks as these?
> This small inheritance my father left me
> Contenteth me, and worth a monarchy.
> I seek not to wax great by others' waning,
> Or gather wealth, I care not with what envy.
> Sufficeth that I have maintains my state
> And sends the poor well pleasèd from my gate.
> (IV.x.18-25)

Iden is reaffirming his resolve to continue living as he does now, away from the turmoil of the court.

Evidences of Resolution-speech can also be found in much more mature soliloquies of Shakespeare, as in key phrases of resolve in Lady Macbeth's two successive soliloquies in the first act of *Macbeth* (v.1-31 and v. 39-55), phrases such as:

> Hie thee hither,
> That I may pour my spirits in thine ear,
> And chastise with the valor of my tongue
> All that impedes thee from the golden round
> (11. 26-29)

and especially in her:

> Come, you spirits
> That tend on mortal thoughts, unsex me here,
> And fill me, from the crown to the toe, topfull
> Of direst cruelty! Make thick my blood,
> Stop up the accéss and passage to remorse,
> That no compunctious visitings of nature
> Shake my fell purpose, nor keep peace between
> The effect and it! (11. 41-48)

While the two soliloquies of Lady Macbeth cited here would not be classifiable primarily as Resolution-speeches, they do indicate, as Clemen declares, that "within the compass of Shakespeare's work we can trace the development of the . . . resolution-speech from primitive state to more complex and mature forms."[3]

Another medieval convention prominently reflected in early Shakespeare is the Lament soliloquy, demonstrated in Chapter iii to have been a regular feature of morality plays, and analyzed in Chapter v as an emotive type in Shakespeare. Laments appear frequently in the author's early plays; perhaps his best known variety is the king's lament on the loneliness of royal position, exemplified in speeches by Henry VI (II.v.1-54 of Part III — examined later in this chapter for extravagances of language), Henry V (IV.i.247-301 — "We must bear all"), and Henry IV (*II Henry IV:* III.i.4-31), the most famous king's lament in Shakespeare ("Uneasy lies the head that wears a crown"). There are also the Laments to Grief or Woe, such as that of Titus on the Tribunes' condemnation of his two sons (III.i.12-22), and Wolsey's in *Henry VIII* on the loss of his greatness (III.ii.350-72). (The last mentioned comes of course at the end of Shakespeare's career, not at or near the beginning like the other laments noted here.) And, finally, there is the Death-lament of Lord Clifford in *III Henry VI* (II.vi.1-30), analyzed at length, like others of the above, in Chapter v.

Close dependence on medieval types is only one of the two main demonstrations of primitiveness in early Shakespearean soliloquy. The other, extravagances in language, is probably more visible to twentieth-century readers. Concerning such extravagances, Senecan influence on the rhetoric of Shakespeare's early drama is a foregone conclusion of most present-day criticism. The furiousness of Seneca's heroes is seldom, perhaps not at all emulated by Shakespeare's personae, but the other excesses of Seneca's now amusingly flowery and figurative language often appear in early Shakespeare plays: a great number of extravagantly rhetorical soliloquies are in the plays written before 1600 (and there are some in plays written later). In *The Oration in Shakespeare*, p. 41, Kennedy says, "Titus [the character] affords probably the best vehicle in Shakespeare, with the possible exception of Timon, for the use of sophistic rhetoric of the melodramatic kind." Aaron, not Titus, however, offers prime instance of Senecan language in soliloquy in that play, in his speech opening Act II (i.1-24):

> Now climbeth Tamora Olympus' top,
> Safe out of Fortune's shot, and sits aloft,
> Secure of thunder's crack or lightning flash,
> Advanced above pale envy's threatening reach.
> As when the golden sun salutes the morn,
> And, having gilt the ocean with his beams,
> Gallops the zodiac in his glistering coach,
> And overlooks the highest-peering hills,
> So Tamora.
> Upon her wit doth earthly honor wait,
> And virtue stoops and trembles at her frown.
> Then, Aaron, arm thy heart, and fit thy thoughts,
> To mount aloft with thy imperial mistress,
> And mount her pitch, whom thou in triumph long
> Hast prisoner held, fettered in amorous chains,
> And faster bound to Aaron's charming eyes
> Than is Prometheus tied to Caucasus.
> Away with slavish weeds and servile thoughts!
> I will be bright and shine in pearl and gold,
> To wait upon this new-made Empress.
> To wait, said I? To wanton with this Queen,
> This goddess, this Semiramis, this nymph,
> This siren, that will charm Rome's Saturnine,
> And see his shipwreck and his commonweal's.
>
> (II.i.1-24)

The speech is overflowing with figurative expression — for example, personifications of fortune, envy, and the sun in four successive lines of the opening five, and an intricate metaphor of the sun's saluting the morn, gilding the ocean, galloping its course and overlooking the highest hills — all within the opening nine lines. Classical allusion, the effusive likening of Tamora to the sun, and images of falconry, pearl and gold all add to the impression that the language was intended primarily as "declamation and display."[4]

A second such instance of Senecan qualities in early Shakespearean soliloquy occurs in the speech by King Henry opening Scene v of the second act in *III Henry VI* (analyzed in part as lament in Chapter vii):

> This battle fares like to the morning's war,
> When dying clouds contend with growing light,
> What time the shepherd, blowing of his nails,
> Can neither call it perfect day or night.
> Now sways it this way, like a mighty sea
> Forced by the tide to combat with the wind.

Now sways it that way, like the selfsame sea
Forced to retire by fury of the wind.
Sometime the flood prevails, and then the wind,
Now one the better, then another best,
Both tugging to be victors, breast to breast,
Yet neither conqueror nor conquerèd:
So is the equal poise of this fell war.
Here on this molehill will I sit me down.
To whom God will, there be the victory!
For Margaret my Queen, and Clifford too,
Have chid me from the battle, swearing both
They prosper best of all when I am thence.
Would I were dead, if God's good will were so,
For what is in this world but grief and woe?
Oh, God! Methinks it were a happy life
To be no better than a homely swain,
To sit upon a hill, as I do now,
To carve out dials quaintly, point by point,
Thereby to see the minutes how they run —
How many make the hour full complete,
How many hours bring about the day,
How many days will finish up the year,
How many years a mortal man may live.
When this is known, then to divide the times —
So many hours must I tend my flock,
So many hours must I take my rest,
So many hours must I contemplate.
So many hours must I sport myself;
So many days my ewes have been with young,
So many weeks ere the poor fools will ean,
So many years ere I shall shear the fleece.
So minutes, hours, days, months, and years,
Passed over to the end they were created,
Would bring white hairs unto a quiet grave.
Ah, what a life were this! How sweet! How lovely!
Gives not the hawthorn bush a sweeter shade
To shepherds looking on their silly sheep
Than doth a rich embroidered canopy
To kings that fear their subjects' treachery?
Oh, yes, it doth, a thousandfold it doth.
And to conclude, the shepherd's homely curds,
His cold thin drink out of his leather bottle,
His wonted sleep under a fresh tree's shade,
All which secure and sweetly he enjoys,
Is far beyond a prince's delicates,
His viands sparkling in a golden cup,

His body couchèd in a curious bed,
When care, mistrust, and treason waits on him.
(II.v.1-54)

Henry's speech exemplifies piling-on of images, one after another. It labors in catachresis, as in the "morning's war" metaphor which stretches out to occupy an entire twelve lines of the speech in a rocking rhythm of "now one, then another" contraries just short of absurd when compared to Shakespeare's use of contraries in many speeches in later plays. The sense of much of the speech is circumscribed by exact rhyming of end-stopped lines. The repetition of "How many" which opens four successive lines (26-29) and of the answering "So many" opening seven more (31-37) is a device soon abandoned by Shakespeare for the remainder of his career. Indeed, in comparison to the laments of later Shakespearean kings on the loneliness of the crown, only in its final lines (41-54) would the soliloquy elicit from audiences (either readers or listeners, Elizabethan or modern) that sympathy for the lonely leader which seems to be (other than mere declamation) the purpose of the oration.

Before examing sophistication in later Shakespearean soliloquies, it should be reiterated that an admixture of primitive and sophisticated elements is the rule, not the exception, throughout the pre-1600 speeches. The first soliloquy cited in this chapter, spoken by Richard, Duke of Gloucester in *III Henry VI* (III.ii.124-95), represents an isolated instance of Shakespeare's beginning to break away from primitive excesses in language even in his very first plays.[5]

Later Sophistication

According to Harrison, p. 809, *Julius Caesar* was written in 1599; from this play is excerpted an opening example of the refinement in later Shakespearean soliloquy. As explained at the outset of the chapter, this sophistication involves originality of structure and diction not usually present in the so-called primitive soliloquies of Shakespeare's earliest dramas, depends much less on elaborately figurative language or on rhyme, and approximates the rhythms and wording of spontaneous — as distinguished from formally rhetorical — speaking.

Brutus speaks three soliloquies in quick succession as the second act opens in *Caesar*. The gist of the first lies in the remark:

He would be crowned.
How that might change his nature, there's the question.
(II.i.12-13)

Jorgensen is of the opinion, concerning this speech, that "Shakespeare is here on the road to Hamlet's great soliloquy."[6] The third soliloquy of Brutus' series of three is his address to Conspiracy, a speech almost entirely dependent on a rhetorical device, the personification of Conspiracy. However, the second of the three soliloquies is offered here as example of sophistication in soliloquy. It too depends, in one sense, on a figure of speech, that of man as microcosm within macrocosm, a familiar Elizabethan conceit. But its basic quality is that of effective expression of a very ordinary experience shared by all men, the experience of that horrible waiting period between decision and action on fateful questions:

> Since Cassius first did whet me against Caesar
> I have not slept.
> Between the acting of a dreadful thing
> And the first motion, all the interim is
> Like a phantasma or a hideous dream.
> The Genius and the mortal instruments
> Are then in council, and the state of man,
> Like to a little kingdom, suffers then
> The nature of an insurrection. (II.i.61-69)

Given the tendency to figurative language in Elizabethan drama, and the apparent ability of Elizabethan audiences to decipher and appreciate that figurativeness, the conciseness of this little speech is remarkable. Granted also the ready comprehension in Shakespeare's contemporary audiences that the playwright was writing here on the influence of the mind on man's physical state (Genius=soul; instruments=body: together they prevent sleep, as in a kingdom rent by civil war), Brutus' language is as plain as can be, especially heightened in its clarity by such words as "hideous," "little kingdom," "suffers" and the highly charged "insurrection." In contrast to the postures often struck by kings delivering soliloquies in his histories, Shakespeare depicts Brutus in one key line: "I have not slept," and has him proceed to reveal precisely why.

As previously iterated, not all of the sophistication in soliloquy is found in the later works. One example of earlier independence in structure and diction is the famous Honor speech by Falstaff, spoken in response to Hal's "Why, thou owest God a death." Falstaff's answer:

> 'Tis not due yet, I would be loath to pay Him before his day. What need I be so forward with him that calls not on me? Well, 'tis no matter. Honor pricks me on. Yea, but how if honor prick me off when I come on? How then? Can honor set to a leg? No. Or an arm? No. Or take away the grief of a wound? No. Honor hath no skill in surgery, then? No. What is honor? A word. What is in that word honor? What is that honor? Air. A trim reckoning! Who hath it? He that died o' Wednesday. Doth he feel it? No. Doth he hear it? No. 'Tis insensible, then? Yea, to the dead. But will it not live with the living? No. Why? Detraction will not suffer it. Therefore I'll

none of it. Honor is a mere scutcheon. And so ends my catechism. (V.i.127-43)[7]

Originality in structure appears in the fact that, while on the surface Falstaff's reply is comic in tone (and somewhat in diction, too), its underlying tone is seriousness — Sir John is "kidding on the square" here; a woeful sentiment is cloaked in robes of comic speech. In truth, Falstaff is portrayed as quite contemplative in some of the lines, as in

> Yea, but how if honor prick me off when I come on? How then? (131-32)

The speech is replete with imagery, fiscal at the opening, and of swordsmanship and surgery later on. But reliance on images only enhances the meanings of the speech, as especially in the last image of all:

> Honor is a mere scutcheon. (143)

The speech is also, in toto, a homily as witness its conclusive lines:

> But will it not live with the living? No. Why? Detraction [slander] will not suffer it. (140-42)

As for originality of diction, Falstaff speaks with the plainness and clarity of Hamlet or Edmund, and in terms familiar to all, Elizabethan or present-day American. Such plain-speaking is not representative of most Shakespearean soliloquies before 1600, but is characteristic of soliloquy sophistication usually expected (and found) in the later great tragedies. (Harrison states, p. 613, that the play was "probably written in the autumn of 1597.")

Hal's "I know you all, and will a while uphold . . ." speech (I.ii.218-40), although rather on the rhetorical side of early soliloquies, offers, in the same play, at least a strong inkling of the spontaneity of speaking of the later tragedies, in the Prince's brusquely candid assessment of his situation vis-à-vis the roughneck band of which he is presently a part. It is, however, not sufficiently representative of sophistication to warrant full examination here.

Shakespeare's need to represent spontaneity in the speaking of such later personae as, say, Hamlet led to the aforementioned originality of structure and diction, to a different kind of verse (i.e., tended to "break down the form of the verse"),[8] and that very breaking-down (change) constituted a more direct, realistic expression of character and emotion, especially for such roles as Hamlet. By "spontaneous" is of course meant a semblance of spontaneity, because the true spontaneity of colloquial talk is probably never to be found in Elizabethan soliloquy, nor was it meant to be. Even the words of Petruchio in the following excerpt from *The Taming of the Shrew*, seemingly so completely colloquial, are iambics, so suitable for setting to music that Cole Porter did just that in *Kiss Me, Kate*. Here,

Shakespeare:

> And if she chance to nod, I'll rail and brawl,
> And with the clamor keep her still awake.
> This is a way to kill a wife with kindness.
>
> (IV.i.209-11)

For that matter, in modern plays as highly acclaimed for realism in dialogue as *All My Sons* or *Streetcar Named Desire*, the speaking also represents a playwright's careful selection of cogent words, not the unorganized redundancy of most natural talking, as the most colloquial sounding of Robert Frost's poems are verse, not natural speech.

Spontaneous qualities in Hamlet's soliloquies are an obvious fact, probably the epitome of seeming spontaneity in dramatic dialogue. This fact has already been dealt with in Chapter v in regard to the "realism" of imagery in Hamlet's fourth. To avoid laboring the obvious, the concluding portion of this chapter focuses on soliloquies in other of the later plays, which speeches also demonstrate qualities of naturalistic speaking and thus bespeak evolution within Shakespearean soliloquy.

A soliloquy displaying naturalness approximating that of non-stage speech is spoken by Edmund in the second scene of *Lear*. It is in prose, although full of bountiful Elizabethan periods, triadic repetitions, and a rolling, relentless rhythm putting it notably close to poetry, if not to blank verse per se. It is also, of course, a little homily on man's tendency to explain away his own failings in terms of bad luck (and perhaps a Shakespearean refutation of pre-destination theory as well). But, at this point, most interesting in this speech is its exemplification of the type of plain-speaking soliloquy Shakespeare developed in some of his later works, as in the sample from Brutus earlier in this chapter. Edmund's speech:

> This is the excellent foppery of the world, that when we are sick in fortune — often the surfeit of our own behavior — we make guilty of our disasters the sun, the moon, and the stars, as if we were villains by necessity, fools by heavenly compulsion; knaves, thieves, and treachers by spherical predominance; drunkards, liars, and adulterers by an enforced obedience of planetary influence; and all that we are evil in, by a divine thrusting on — an admirable evasion of whoremaster man, to lay his goatish disposition to the charge of a star! My father compounded with my mother under the dragon's tail, and my nativity was under Ursa Major, so that it follows I am rough and lecherous. Tut, I should have been that I am had the maidenliest star in the firmament twinkled on my bastardizing. (I.ii.128-45)

This is plain-speaking indeed. The portrayal demands it, and Shakespeare is more than equal to the demand. Dramatic requirements had become different at this later time in his life; apparent spontaneity of speaking was one of those requirements. Edmund's diction is full of earthy terms; its terms are definite, forceful, blunt ("foppery," "evasion," "goatish"). The speech approaches the pinnacle of Shakespeare's presentation of spontaneous utterance on the stage.

Last of all, a famed soliloquy in *Macbeth* also affords a clear sampling of spontaneity of speaking. It is Macbeth's final soliloquy:

> Seyton! — I am sick at heart,
> When I behold — Seyton, I say! — This push
> Will cheer me ever or disseat me now.
> I have lived long enough. My way of life
> Is fall'n into the sear, the yellow leaf,
> And that which should accompany old age,
> As honor, love, obedience, troops of friends,
> I must not look to have, but in their stead
> Curses, not loud but deep, mouth-honor, breath,
> Which the poor heart would fain deny, and dare not.
>   (V.iii.19-28)

Macbeth's images of autumn leaves, and his listing of the irrevocably forsaken accouterments of a gracious old age, might well be described in the same words Clemen has employed in reviewing the imagery of Hamlet: "easy to understand; common and ordinary things, things familiar to the man in the street."[9] There is nothing in the soliloquy of Macbeth which would give even a moment's pause to the groundlings at The Globe, or even to members, however unlearned, of a present-day audience. Macbeth's declaration, to be sure, is poetry; it is fairly regularized blank verse. Marlowe's mighty line has evolved into the writing of character-speech at once figurative and down-to-earth, and so unmistakable in meaning as to seem like ordinary speech. "Ordinary speaking" is demanded by the subject-matter of the play, in this case the meditativeness of a "real" man fallen from former grace and noblesse, as contrasted to poetic posturings suitable for fallen kings in romantic chronicle plays. Macbeth's lament attains to the heights of sophistication to be seen within Shakespeare's evolution as a writer of soliloquy.

The findings of this concluding chapter, exploring evolution within the body of Shakespearean soliloquy, serve only to reinforce the central thesis of this study. That is, the culmination of English soliloquy in a few of Shakespeare's finest offerings is only the crowning phase in an evolutionary development commencing in Athenian, Roman, and even earlier drama, beginning again, as it were, in the Mysteries and Moralities of England, eventually hearkening back to the classical foundations during the drama immediately preceding Shakespeare, and continually evident within his own efforts.

Notes

Chapter VI

[1] Harley Granville-Barker, *Prefaces to Shakespeare* (London: 1948), II, 277.

[2] Clemen, *Tragedy*, pp. 51-52 and passim.

[3] Clemen, *Tragedy*, pp. 51-52.

[4] Kennedy, p. 10. Kennedy points out an evolutionary development of Shakespearean soliloquy but uses the term "oration," a concept broader for Kennedy than "soliloquy" but inclusive of the latter term.

[5] Mahood also emphasizes the earliness of Shakespeare's progression out of primitiveness: ". . . while the personages in his earliest plays speak in Senecan *sententiae*, or Thoughts, the manner of speech of his characters soon changes to what Coleridge called 'I Thinking'". *Wordplay*, p. 19.

[6] Paul A. Jorgensen, *Lear's Self-Discovery* (Berkeley: 1967), p. 57.

[7] There seem to be irregularities in Harrison's numbering of the lines in this speech — indeed, in this edition.

[8] Granville-Barker, *Prefaces*, II, 277.

[9] Clemen, *Imagery*, p. 107.

A Selected Bibliography

Adams, Joseph Quincy. *Chief Pre-Shakespearean Dramas.* Boston: 1924.
Aeschylus' Plays. Trans. Gilbert Murray. 7 vols. New York: 1930.
Aeschylus, The Suppliant Women. Trans. Gilbert Murray. New York: 1935.
Allen, J. T. *Stage Antiquities of the Greeks and Romans.* New York: 1927.
Aristotle the Poetics, "Longinus" On the Sublime, Demetrius, On Style. Loeb Classical Library. Ed. E. Capps, T. E. Page and W. H. D. Rouse. London: 1927.
Arnott, Peter D. *Three Greek Plays for the Theatre.* [Euripides' *Medea, Cyclops,* Aristophanes' *JThe Frogs*] Bloomington, Ind.: 1961.
Arthur Miller's Collected Plays. New York: 1957.
Axton, Richard. *European Drama of the Early Middle Ages.* Pittsburgh: 1975.
Bain, David. *Actors and Audience: a Study of Asides and Related Conventions in Greek Drama.* New York: 1977.
Bamber, Linda. *Comic Women, Tragic Men: A Study of Gender and Genre in Shakespeare.* Stanford: 1982.
Beare, W. *The Roman Stage.* London: 1950.
Bentley, Eric. *The Life of the Drama.* New York: 1964.
Bevington, David. *From Mankind to Marlowe.* Cambr.: 1962.
Bevington, David, comp. *Medieval Drama.* Boston: 1975.
Bible, The. King James Version. 1895; rpt. Philadelphia: 1943.
Bibliography of European Literature. Barron's Educational Series. Ed. V. F. Hopper and Bernard D. N. Grebanier. Brooklyn: 1954.
Bibliography of Medieval Drama. 2nd ed. rev. and enl. Ed. Carl Joseph Stratman. New York: 1972.
Bieber, Margarete. *The History of the Greek and Roman Theater.* 2nd ed. rev. Princeton: 1961.
Blissett, Wm. "The Secret'st Man of Blood. A Study of Dramatic Irony in Macbeth." *Shakespeare Quarterly,* X (Summer, 1959), 397-408.
Bluestone, Max, and Rabkin, Norman, eds. *Shakespeare's Contemporaries.* Englewood Cliffs, N.J.: 1970.
Bock, Philip K. *Shakespeare and Elizabethan Culture: An Anthropological View.* New York: 1984.
Bonner, S. F. *Roman Declamation in the Late Republic and Early Empire.* Berkeley: 1949.
Bradbrook, Muriel C. *Elizabethan Stage Conditions: A Study of Their Place in the Interpretation of Shakespeare's Plays.* Cambr., Engl.: 1932.
Bradley, A. C. *Shakespearean Tragedy.* 2nd ed., 1904; rpt. London: 1949.
Brooke, C. F. Tucker, ed. *The Works of Christopher Marlowe.* 1910; rpt. Ox-

ford: 1969.
Brooks, Cleanth. "The Naked Babe and the Cloak of Manliness," *The Well Wrought Urn*. New York: 1947.
Brown, Ivor. *First Player: the Origin of Drama*. New York: 1928.
Brown, John R. *Shakespeare and His Theatre*. New York: 1982.
Bush, Geoffrey. *Shakespeare and the Natural Condition*. Cambr.: 1956.
Butler, H. E. *Post-Augustan Poetry: from Seneca to Juvenal*. Oxford: 1909.
Butler, James H. *The Theatre and Drama of Greece and Rome*. San Francisco: 1972.
Campbell, Lily B. *Shakespeare's Tragic Heroes: Slaves of Passion*. New York: 1930.
Campbell, O. J. "Shakespeare and the 'New Critics'" *Joseph Quincy Adams: Memorial Studies*. Washington: 1948, pp· 81-96.
Cargill, Oscar. *Drama and Liturgy*. New York: 1930.
Chambers, E. K. *The Mediaeval Stage*. 2 vols. Oxford: 1903.
Charlton, H. B. *Shakespearean Tragedy*. 1947; rpt. Cambr., Engl.: 1961.
Charney, Maurice. *Shakespeare's Roman Plays*. Cambr.: 1961.
The Chester Plays. re-edited from the MSS by the late Dr. Hermann Deimling. London: 1893.
Clemen, Wolfgang. *The Development of Shakespeare's Imagery*. Cambr.: 1951 (orig. publ. in German, 1936).
───. *English Tragedy Before Shakespeare*. Trans. T. S. Dorsch. London: 1961.
───. *Shakespeare's Soliloquies*. 1964; rpt. Folcroft, Pa.: 1977.
Clift, Evelyn H. *Latin Pseudepigrapha: a study in literary attributions*. Baltimore: 1945.
Coleridge, Samuel T. *Shakespearean Criticism* (1811-34). Ed. T. M. Raysor. 2 vols. Cambr.: 1960.
The Complete Greek Drama. Ed. Whitney J. Oates and Eugene O'Neill, Jr. 2 vols. New York: 1938.
The Complete Greek Tragedies. Sophocles — II. Ed. David Grene and Richard Lattimore. Chicago: 1957.
Cooper, Lane, ed. *Fifteen Greek Plays*. Trans. Gilbert Murray et al. New York: 1943.
Cope, Jackson I. *The Theater and the Dream: from Metaphor to Form in Renaissance Drama*. Baltimore: 1973.
Craig, Hardin. *The Enchanted Glass: the Elizabethan Mind in Literature*. 1935; rpt. New York: 1952.
Craik, T. W. *The Tudor Interlude*. London: 1962.
Cruttwell, Patrick. *The Shakespearean Moment and Its Place in the Poetry of the Seventeenth Century*. 1954; rpt. New York: 1960.
Curry, Walter Clyde. *Shakespeare's Philosophical Patterns*. Baton Rouge: 1937.
Danby John F. *Shakespeare's Doctrine of Nature: A Study of "King Lear"*. London: 1949.
The Dartmouth Bible. 2nd ed., rev. and enl. Ed. Roy B. Chamberlin and

Herman Feldman. Boston: 1961.
Davis, N., ed. *Non-Cycle Plays and Fragments*. EETS. Oxford: 1970.
Dickey, Franklin W. *Not Wisely But Too Well: Shakespeare's Love Tragedies*. San Marino: 1957.
Dodsley, Robert. *A Select Collection of Old English Plays*. 4th ed. by W. Carew Hazlitt. 15 vols. 1874-76 (orig. publ. 1744); rpt. New York: 1964.
Donaldson, John W. *The Theatre of the Greeks*. 8th ed. London: 1875.
Dowden, Edward. *Shakespere: A Critical Study of His Mind and Art*. 1875; rpt. New York: 1962.
Driver, Tom. *The Sense of History in Greek and Shakespearean Drama*. New York: 1960.
Duckworth, George E., ed. *The Complete Roman Drama*. 2 vols. New York: 1942.
——————. *The Nature of Roman Comedy, a study in popular entertainment*. Princeton: 1952.
Duff, J. Wight. *Roman Satire: Its Outlook on Social Life*. Berkeley: 1936.
Dunn, Esther C., ed. *Eight Famous Elizabethan Plays*. New York: 1950.
Eliot, T. S. *Elizabethan Essays*. New York: 1964.
Elliott, G. R. *Dramatic Providence in "Macbeth"*. Princeton: 1958.
——————. *Flaming Minister: a Study of "Othello"*. Durham: 1953.
——————. *Scourge and Minister: a Study of "Hamlet" as a Tragedy of Revengefulness and Justice*. Durham: 1951.
Elton, Wm. *King Lear and the Gods*. San Marino: 1960.
Empson, Wm. *The Structure of Complex Words*. Ann Arbor: 1967.
English Morality Plays and Moral Interludes. Ed. Edgar T. Schell and J. D. Shuchter. New York: 1969.
Erickson, Peter B. "Sexual Politics and the Social Structure in *As You Like It*." *Mass. Review*, 23 (Spring, 1982), 65-83.
Euripides II. Great Books of the Western World, Vol. 5. Trans. Edw. P. Coleridge. London: 1904.
Euripides, Orestes and Other Plays. Penguin Classics. Trans. Philip Vellacott. Harmondsworth: 1972.
Euripides, the Plays. Trans. Gilbert Murray. 2 vols. London: 1911.
Farmer, John S., ed. *Early English Dramatists: Recently Recovered "Lost" Tudor Plays*. 1907; rpt. New York: 1966.
——————, ed. *John Bale*. 1907; rpt. New York: 1966.
——————, ed. *Six Anonymous Plays* (first series c. 1510-37). 1905; rpt. New York: 1966.
Farnham, Willard. *The Medieval Heritage of Elizabethan Tragedy*. Oxford: 1963.
——————. *Shakespeare's Tragic Frontier: the World of His Final Tragedies*. Berkeley: 1950.
Fergusson, Francis. *Shakespeare: the Pattern in His Carpet*. New York: 1970.
Fluchère, Henri. *Shakespeare: dramaturge élisabéthain*. Trans. Guy Hamilton. New York: 1953.

Fraser, Russell A. *Shakespeare's Poetics in Relation to "King Lear"*. London: 1962.
Frye, Northrop. *Fools of Time: Studies in Shakespearian Tragedy*. Toronto: 1967.
Frye, Roland M. *Shakespeare: The Art of the Dramatist*. Winchester, Mass.: 1981.
Gardiner, H. C. *Mysteries' End*. New Haven: 1946.
Gassner, John. *Form and Idea in Modern Theatre*. New York: 1956.
Gaster, Theodor H. *Thespis; ritual, myth and drama in the ancient Near East*. New York: 1950.
Goddard, Harold. *The Meaning of Shakespeare*. Chicago: 1951.
Granville-Barker, Harley. *Prefaces to Shakespeare*. 2 vols. London: 1948.
Gurr, Andrew. *Shakespearean Stage: 1574-1642*. 2nd ed. Cambr., Engl.: 1981.
Harbage, Alfred. *Shakespeare's Audience*. New York: 1941.
Harrison, G. B., ed. *Shakespeare: the Complete Works*. New York: 1968.
Harrison, Jane. *Prologomena to the Study of Greek Religion*. Cambr.: 1921.
Heilman, Robert B., ed. *An Anthology of English Drama Before Shakespeare*. New York: 1952.
——————. *Magic in the Web: Action and Language in "Othello"*. Lexington: 1956.
——————. *Shakespeare: The Tragedies; Twentieth Century Views, New Perspectives*. Des Moines: 1984.
——————. *This Great Stage: Image and Structure in "King Lear"*. Baton Rouge: 1948.
Henderson, Philip, ed. *The Complete Poems of John Skelton*. 2nd, rev. ed. London and Toronto: 1948.
Heuer, Herman. "From Plutarch to Shakespeare: A Study of *Coriolanus*." Shakespeare Survey 10 (1957), 50-59.
Hinman, Charlton, ed. *The First Folio of Shakespeare: the Norton Facsimile*. New York: 1968.
Hodges, C. Walter. *Shakespeare's Theatre*. New York: 1980.
Holloway, John. *The Story of the Night: Studies in Shakespeare's Major Tragedies*. Lincoln, Nebr.: 1961.
Holmes, Martin. *Shakespeare and Burbage: The Sound of Shakespeare as Devised to Suit the Voice and Talent of His Principal Player*. Totowa, N. J.: 1978.
Hulme, Hilda M. *Explorations in Shakespeare's Language*. London: 1962.
Hunningher, Benjamin. *The Origin of the Theater: an Essay*. New York: 1955.
Jones, Ernest. *Hamlet and Oedipus*. New York: 1949.
Jorgensen, Paul A. *Lear's Self-Discovery*. Berkeley: 1967.
Joseph, B. L. *Elizabethan Acting*. London: 1951.
Kennedy, Milton B. *The Oration in Shakespeare*. Chapel Hill: 1942.
Kermode, Frank, ed. *Four Centuries of Shakespearian Criticism*. New York: 1965.

Kirkwood, Gordon M. *Early Greek Monody: the History of a Poetic Type.* Ithaca: 1974.
Kitto, H. D. F. *Form and Meaning in Drama: A Study of Six Greek Plays and of "Hamlet".* 2nd ed. London: 1964.
Klein, David. *The Elizabethan Dramatists as Critics.* New York: 1963.
Knight, G. Wilson. *The Wheel of Fire.* 1930; rpt. London: 1959.
Knights, L. C. *Some Shakespearean Themes.* Stanford: 1960.
Kott, Jan. *Shakespeare Our Contemporary.* Trans. B. Taborski. Garden City, N. Y.: 1964.
Kyd, Thomas. *The Spanish Tragedy.* Ed. Charles T. Prouty. New York: 1951.
Lawlor, John. *The Tragic Sense in Shakespeare.* New York: 1960.
Leider, Emily W. "Plainness of Style in *King Lear.*" *Shakespeare Quarterly,* XXI (Winter, 1970), 45-53.
Levin, Harry. *The Question of Hamlet.* Oxford: 1959.
The Literature of England. Ed. George K. Anderson and Wm. E. Buckler. 5th ed. 2 vols. Glenview, Ill.: 1966.
The Loeb Classical Library. Ed. E. Capps, T. E. Page, and W. H. D. Rouse. London: 1930. [For the classical drama in general.]
Loomis, Roger S., ed. *Representative Medieval and Tudor Plays, Translated and Modernized.* New York: 1942.
MacCallum, M. W. *Shakespeare's Roman Plays and Their Background.* 1910; rpt. London: 1967.
Mack, Maynard. *"King Lear" in Our Time.* Berkeley: 1965.
─────────. "The World of *Hamlet.*" *Yale Review,* XLI (1952), 502-23.
Mahood, Molly. *Shakespeare's Wordplay.* London: 1957.
Manly, John M., ed. *Specimens of the Pre-Shaksperean Drama.* 3 vols. Boston: 1925.
Matthews, H. M. V. *Character and Symbol in Shakespeare's Plays.* Cambr., Engl.: 1962.
Maxwell, J. C. "Animal Imagery in *Coriolanus.*" *Modern Language Review,* XLII (1947), 417-21.
McAdam, E. L., Jr., and George Milne. *Johnson's Dictionary.* New York: 1963.
Medieval Mysteries, Moralities, and Interludes. Ed. Vincent F. Hopper and Gerald B. Lahey. Great Neck, N. Y.: 1962.
Murray, Gilbert. "Hamlet and Orestes: A Study in Traditional Types." *Proceedings of the British Academy, 1913-14.* 4th Annual Shakespeare Lecture. London: 1914.
Nagler, A. M. *Shakespeare's Stage.* New Haven: 1981.
Norwood, Gilbert. *Plautus and Terence.* New York: 1932.
Oliver, H. J. "Coriolanus as Tragic Hero." *Shakespeare Quarterly,* X (Winter, 1959), 52-58.
O'Neill, Eugene. *More Stately Mansions.* Ed. Donald Gallup. New Haven: 1964.
Ovid. *Metamorphoses.* Trans. Rolfe Humphries. Bloomington, Ind.: 1955.

Paul, Henry N. *The Royal Play of "Macbeth": When, Why, and How It Was Written by Shakespeare.* New York: 1951.
Perspectives of Roman Poetry: A Classics Symposium. Symposia in the Art & Humanities. No. 1. Ed. G. Karl Galinsky. Austin: 1974.
Phillips, James E., Jr. *The State in Shakespeare's Greek and Roman Plays.* New York: 1940.
Plautus. Loeb Classical Library. Trans. Paul Nixon. Cambr.: 1950-52.
Plautus: Rudens and Other Plays. Broadway Transl. Series. Trans. F. A. Wright and H. L. Rogers. London: n.d.
Plautus: Three Comedies. Trans. Erich Segal. New York: 1969.
Proser, Matthew N. *The Heroic Image in Five Shakespearean Tragedies.* Princeton: 1965.
Quiller-Couch, Arthur. *Shakespeare's Workmanship.* 1918; rpt. Cambr., Engl.: 1931.
Rabkin, Norman. *Shakespeare and the Common Understanding.* New York: 1967.
Ribner, Irving, ed. *Christopher Marlowe's "Doctor Faustus": Text and Major Criticism.* New York: 1966.
——————. *Patterns in Shakespearean Tragedy.* London: 1960.
Righter, Anne. *Shakespeare and the Idea of the Play.* London: 1964.
Rodriguez Adrados, Francisco. *Festival, Comedy and Tragedy: the Greek Origins of Theatre.* Trans. Christopher Holme. Leiden: 1975.
Rosen, Wm. *Shakespeare and the Craft of Tragedy.* Cambr.: 1960.
Rosenberg, Marvin. *The Masks of Othello.* Berkeley: 1961.
Rossiter, A. P. *English Drama from the Early Times to the Elizabethans.* London: 1950.
Ruth, Carolyn, et al. *The Woman's Part: Feminist Criticism of Shakespeare.* Champaign, Ill.: 1980.
Schucking, Levin L. *Character Problems in Shakespeare's Plays.* New York: 1922.
Segal, Erich W. *Roman Laughter; the Comedy of Plautus.* Cambr.: 1968.
Sellar, W. Y. *The Roman Poets of the Republic.* New edit., rev. and enl. Oxford: 1881.
Seneca, His Tenne Tragedies Translated into English. Ed. Thomas Newton. 1581; rpt. Bloomington, Ind.: n.d.
Seneca. *Thyestes.* Trans. Moses Hadas. Indianapolis: 1957.
The Seven Against Thebes. Oxford Univ. Press Series. Trans. Gilbert Murray. New York: 1935.
Sewall, Richard B. *The Vision of Tragedy.* New Haven: 1959.
Siegel, Paul N. *Shakespearean Tragedy and the Elizabethan Compromise.* New York: 1957.
Sisson, C. J. *Shakespeare's Tragic Justice.* London: 1962.
Speaight, Robert. *Shakespeare: The Man and His Achievement.* Briarcliff Manor, N. Y.: 1982.
Spencer, Theodore. *Shakespeare and the Nature of Man.* 2nd ed. New York: 1949.

Kirkwood, Gordon M. *Early Greek Monody: the History of a Poetic Type.* Ithaca: 1974.

Kitto, H. D. F. *Form and Meaning in Drama: A Study of Six Greek Plays and of "Hamlet".* 2nd ed. London: 1964.

Klein, David. *The Elizabethan Dramatists as Critics.* New York: 1963.

Knight, G. Wilson. *The Wheel of Fire.* 1930; rpt. London: 1959.

Knights, L. C. *Some Shakespearean Themes.* Stanford: 1960.

Kott, Jan. *Shakespeare Our Contemporary.* Trans. B. Taborski. Garden City, N. Y.: 1964.

Kyd, Thomas. *The Spanish Tragedy.* Ed. Charles T. Prouty. New York: 1951.

Lawlor, John. *The Tragic Sense in Shakespeare.* New York: 1960.

Leider, Emily W. "Plainness of Style in *King Lear.*" *Shakespeare Quarterly,* XXI (Winter, 1970), 45-53.

Levin, Harry. *The Question of Hamlet.* Oxford: 1959.

The Literature of England. Ed. George K. Anderson and Wm. E. Buckler. 5th ed. 2 vols. Glenview, Ill.: 1966.

The Loeb Classical Library. Ed. E. Capps, T. E. Page, and W. H. D. Rouse. London: 1930. [For the classical drama in general.]

Loomis, Roger S., ed. *Representative Medieval and Tudor Plays, Translated and Modernized.* New York: 1942.

MacCallum, M. W. *Shakespeare's Roman Plays and Their Background.* 1910; rpt. London: 1967.

Mack, Maynard. *"King Lear" in Our Time.* Berkeley: 1965.

———. "The World of *Hamlet.*" *Yale Review,* XLI (1952), 502-23.

Mahood, Molly. *Shakespeare's Wordplay.* London: 1957.

Manly, John M., ed. *Specimens of the Pre-Shaksperean Drama.* 3 vols. Boston: 1925.

Matthews, H. M. V. *Character and Symbol in Shakespeare's Plays.* Cambr., Engl.: 1962.

Maxwell, J. C. "Animal Imagery in *Coriolanus.*" *Modern Language Review,* XLII (1947), 417-21.

McAdam, E. L., Jr., and George Milne. *Johnson's Dictionary.* New York: 1963.

Medieval Mysteries, Moralities, and Interludes. Ed. Vincent F. Hopper and Gerald B. Lahey. Great Neck, N. Y.: 1962.

Murray, Gilbert. "Hamlet and Orestes: A Study in Traditional Types." *Proceedings of the British Academy, 1913-14.* 4th Annual Shakespeare Lecture. London: 1914.

Nagler, A. M. *Shakespeare's Stage.* New Haven: 1981.

Norwood, Gilbert. *Plautus and Terence.* New York: 1932.

Oliver, H. J. "Coriolanus as Tragic Hero." *Shakespeare Quarterly,* X (Winter, 1959), 52-58.

O'Neill, Eugene. *More Stately Mansions.* Ed. Donald Gallup. New Haven: 1964.

Ovid. *Metamorphoses.* Trans. Rolfe Humphries. Bloomington, Ind.: 1955.

Paul, Henry N. *The Royal Play of "Macbeth": When, Why, and How It Was Written by Shakespeare.* New York: 1951.
Perspectives of Roman Poetry: A Classics Symposium. Symposia in the Art & Humanities. No. 1. Ed. G. Karl Galinsky. Austin: 1974.
Phillips, James E., Jr. *The State in Shakespeare's Greek and Roman Plays.* New York: 1940.
Plautus. Loeb Classical Library. Trans. Paul Nixon. Cambr.: 1950-52.
Plautus: Rudens and Other Plays. Broadway Transl. Series. Trans. F. A. Wright and H. L. Rogers. London: n.d.
Plautus: Three Comedies. Trans. Erich Segal. New York: 1969.
Proser, Matthew N. *The Heroic Image in Five Shakespearean Tragedies.* Princeton: 1965.
Quiller-Couch, Arthur. *Shakespeare's Workmanship.* 1918; rpt. Cambr., Engl.: 1931.
Rabkin, Norman. *Shakespeare and the Common Understanding.* New York: 1967.
Ribner, Irving, ed. *Christopher Marlowe's "Doctor Faustus": Text and Major Criticism.* New York: 1966.
―――――. *Patterns in Shakespearean Tragedy.* London: 1960.
Righter, Anne. *Shakespeare and the Idea of the Play.* London: 1964.
Rodriguez Adrados, Francisco. *Festival, Comedy and Tragedy: the Greek Origins of Theatre.* Trans. Christopher Holme. Leiden: 1975.
Rosen, Wm. *Shakespeare and the Craft of Tragedy.* Cambr.: 1960.
Rosenberg, Marvin. *The Masks of Othello.* Berkeley: 1961.
Rossiter, A. P. *English Drama from the Early Times to the Elizabethans.* London: 1950.
Ruth, Carolyn, et al. *The Woman's Part: Feminist Criticism of Shakespeare.* Champaign, Ill.: 1980.
Schucking, Levin L. *Character Problems in Shakespeare's Plays.* New York: 1922.
Segal, Erich W. *Roman Laughter; the Comedy of Plautus.* Cambr.: 1968.
Sellar, W. Y. *The Roman Poets of the Republic.* New edit., rev. and enl. Oxford: 1881.
Seneca, His Tenne Tragedies Translated into English. Ed. Thomas Newton. 1581; rpt. Bloomington, Ind.: n.d.
Seneca. *Thyestes.* Trans. Moses Hadas. Indianapolis: 1957.
The Seven Against Thebes. Oxford Univ. Press Series. Trans. Gilbert Murray. New York: 1935.
Sewall, Richard B. *The Vision of Tragedy.* New Haven: 1959.
Siegel, Paul N. *Shakespearean Tragedy and the Elizabethan Compromise.* New York: 1957.
Sisson, C. J. *Shakespeare's Tragic Justice.* London: 1962.
Speaight, Robert. *Shakespeare: The Man and His Achievement.* Briarcliff Manor, N. Y.: 1982.
Spencer, Theodore. *Shakespeare and the Nature of Man.* 2nd ed. New York: 1949.

Spencer, T. J. B. "Shakespeare and The Elizabethan Romans." *Shakespeare Survey 10* (1957), 27-28.

———. *Shakespeare: The Roman Plays*. London: 1963.

Spivack, Bernard. *Shakespeare and the Allegory of Evil: The History of a Metaphor in Relation to His Major Villains*. New York: 1958.

Spurgeon, Caroline. *Shakespeare's Imagery and What It Tells Us*. Cambr., Engl.: 1935.

Stanford, Wm. B. *Aeschylus in His Style: a Study in Language and Personality*. Dublin: 1942.

Stirling, Brents. *Unity in Shakespearian Tragedy: The Interplay of Theme and Character*. New York: 1956.

Stoll, Elmer E. *From Shakespeare to Joyce*. New York: 1944.

Thomson, George. *Aeschylus and Athens*. New York: 1967.

Thrall, Wm. F., et al. *A Handbook to Literature*. Rev. and enl. ed. New York: 1960.

Tillyard, E. M. W. *The Elizabethan World Picture*. New York: 1944.

———. *Shakespeare's History Plays*. London: 1962.

Traversi, D. A. *Shakespeare: The Roman Plays*. Stanford: 1963.

A Treasury of the Theatre. Ed. John Gassner and Bernard Dukore. 4th ed. 2 vols. New York: 1970.

Trousdale, Marion. *Shakespeare and the Rhetoricians*. Chapel Hill: 1982.

Tunison, Joseph S. *Dramatic Traditions of the Dark Ages*. Chicago: 1970.

Twenty-Five Modern Plays. Ed. S. Marion Tucker. 3rd ed. New York: 1953.

Villarejo, O. M. "Shakespeare's *Romeo and Juliet:* Its Spanish Source." *Shakespeare Survey 20* (1967), 95-105.

Waith, Eugene. *The Herculean Hero*. New York: 1962.

Walker, Roy. *The Time Is Free*. London: 1949.

———. *The Time Is Out of Joint: A Study of "Hamlet"*. London: 1948.

Waterhouse, Osborn, ed. *The Non-Cycle Mystery Plays*. EETS. London: 1909.

Watson, C. B. *Shakespeare and the Renaissance Concept of Honor*. Princeton: 1960.

Williamson, Claude C. *Readings on the Character of Hamlet, 1661-1947*. London: 1950.

Wilson, Harold S. *On the Design of Shakespearian Tragedy*. Toronto: 1957.

Wilson, J. Dover. *What Happens in "Hamlet"*. 3rd ed. Cambr., Engl.: 1951.

Wright, F. A. *Three Roman Poets*. New York: 1938.

Young, Karl. *The Drama of the Medieval Church*. 1933; rpt. Oxford: 1951.